Bread
D0764718

101 Production Cookbooks

The Art of Cooking for Two by Coralie Castle & Astrid Newton
Barbecue & Smoke Cookery by Maggie Waldron
Bread & Breakfast by Linda Kay Bistow
The Calculating Cook by Jeanne Jones
Coffee by Kenneth Davids
Espresso by Kenneth Davids
The Ethnic Vegetarian Kitchen by Shanta Nimbark Sacharoff
Fifteen Minute Meals by Emalee Chapman
Flavors of Hungary by Charlotte Slovak Biro
Flavors of India by Shanta Nimbark Sacharoff
Flavors of Mexico by Angeles de la Rosa & C. Gandia de Fernández
Flavors of Northern Italy by Violeta Autumn
Gourmet Garden by Coralie Castle & Robert Kourik
Greek Cooking for the Gods by Eva Zane
Grill It In! by Barbara Grunes
The Home & Grill Cookbook by Barbara Grunes
Hors d'Oeuvre Book by Coralie Castle
Juice It Up! by Patricia Gentry & Lynne Devereux
Kabobs on the Grill by Barbara Grunes
More Calculated Cooking by Jeanne Jones
The New Harvest by Lou Seibert Pappas & Jane Horn
One Pot Meals by Maggie Gin
Pasta International by Gertrude Harris
The Portable Feast by Diane D. MacMillan
Real Bread by Maggie Baylis & Coralie Castle
Secrets of Salt-Free Cooking by Jeanne Jones
Some Like It Hotter by Geraldine Duncann
Soup by Coralie Castle
The Tea Lover's Treasury by James Norwood Pratt
Vegetarian Gourmet Cookery by Alan Hooker
Diet for a Happy Heart by Jeanne Jones
Teatime Celebrations by Patricia Gentry

These titles can be ordered directly from the publisher:
The Cole Group, Inc., 4415 Sonoma Highway, Santa Rosa, CA 95409, (707) 538-0495

They are available at your local bookstores or wholesalers nationwide through:
Publishers Group West, 4065 Hollis, Emeryville, CA 94608, (800) 788-3123

And for gift and gourmet retailers, department stores and housewares merchants through:
Profiles Books, P.O. Box 5553, Kent, WA 98064, (800) 451-7647

In Canada please contact:
McClelland & Stewart, Inc., 380 Esna Park Drive, Markham, Ontario, CAN L3R 1H5
(800) 268-5748, or (800) 268-5707 (from Ontario and Quebec)

Bread & Breakfast

The Best Recipes from North America's Bed & Breakfast Inns

Linda Kay Bristow

Illustrations by
Roy Killeen and Others

101 PRODUCTIONS

Publisher Brete Harrison
Associate Publisher James Connolly
Director of Production Steve Lux
Production Assistant Dotti Hydue
Front and Back Cover photography Dennis Gray
Illustrations Roy Killeen and Others

Text copyright © 1985, 1988, 1993 The Cole Group
Illustrations copyright © 1985, 1988, 1993 The Cole Group

All rights reserved under international and Pan-American copyright conventions. No part of this book may be reproduced in any form without the written permission of the publisher.

Distributed to the book trade by Publishers Group West

Printed and bound in the USA
Published by 101 Productions/The Cole Group
4415 Sonoma Highway, PO Box 4089
Santa Rosa, CA 95402-4089
(707) 538-0492 FAX (707) 538-0497

A B C D E F G H
3 4 5 6 7 8 9 0
Library of Congress Catalog Card Number 92-30279

ISBN 1-56426-551-X

This book is dedicated to the innkeepers who took time out of their busy schedules to write out their recipes, answer endless questions, and encourage my efforts along the way. And to my sister, Angela, whose undying love and unending patience keeps me going.

"The discovery of a new dish does more for the happiness of mankind than the discovery of a star." —Brillat-Savarin

CONTENTS

Some of the drawings in this book have been reproduced from the inns' brochures, with permission of the inns, and are credited to the following artists or sources:

Captain Jefferds, page 5, Judy Logan; Hawthorne Inn, page 7, Gregory Burch; Waybury Inn, page 11, Charles Bergen; The Inn at Manchester, page 15, Anita Sandler; The Inn at Weston, page 16, Robert Bates; Alexander's Inn, page 21; The Mainstay, page 29, Edith Hewitt; The Queen Victoria, page 31, David Pertz; The Summer Cottage Inn, page 35; The Wedgwood Inn, page 37, Carol Stoddard and Leslie Haines; The Greystone Inn, page 46, Sharon Kinnent; The Burn, page 48, Andra Rudolph (reproduced from *Country Inns of the Old South*); Oak Square, page 50, William Williams, Jr.; The Conyers House, page 53, Norman Cartwright-Brown; Thorwood Bed & Breakfast, page 60, Mari Ottersen; The Rahilly House, page 63, Milt Dale; Grant Corner Inn, page 72, Daisy de Puthod; Rose Victorian Inn, page 81, Judith Andreson; Campbell Ranch Inn, page 88, Debra Decker; San Benito House, page 93, Pavesich; Grape Leaf Inn, page 94, Mike Fitzpatrick; The Heirloom, page 96, Helen S. Lambert; The Beazley House, page 98, Melissa Fisher; The Glenborough Inn, page 105, Donna Medley; Romeo Inn, page 113, Gina-Marie Romeo; Pillars by the Sea, page 117, Kay Guthrie & Associates.

Introduction

Who knows breakfast better than the proprietor of a bed and breakfast inn? This was what I asked myself after visiting nearly two hundred of them. And with this thought in mind I set out on a search for the guest-tested, most-requested recipes of North America's favorite innkeepers.

The results were rewarding. Not only did I uncover exciting original recipes, but treasured family favorites (like My Great Aunt Fanny's Date Cake and Grandmother Katarina's Cardamom Bread) and regional specialties as well (Minnesota Wild Rice Waffles and Virginia Ham and Apple Pie).

As with the inns, so with the recipes—the greatest concentrations being found on the east and west coasts. (There was a rousing response from the innkeepers of Cape May, New Jersey, this nation's oldest seaside resort.) And many of their recipes are numbered among my personal favorites, including the Barnard Good House Fresh Peach Soup and the Summer Cottage Torte.

Each recipe in this book has been kitchen tested, and often retested or modified to yield the best possible results. And, as you are about to find out in your own home, each is guaranteed to bring *your* guests back for more.

There is one recipe you won't find here—that's the recipe for the warmth and personal attention of the innkeeper that goes with each meal. As for the inns themselves, all I can hope to do is whet your appetite. To savor the full enjoyment you must visit them yourself. And who knows? Perhaps some morning you and I will meet over Barbados Fruit Medley and Rum-Runner French Toast!

NEW ENGLAND

Butternut Farm
Captain Jefferds Inn
Hawthorne Inn
Holiday Inn
Waybury Inn
The Governor's Inn
The Inn at Manchester
The Inn at Weston

Butternut Farm

Glastonbury, Connecticut

Having called Butternut Farm home for nearly twenty years, Donald Reid decided that it would be highly uncivilized to keep the eighteenth-century farmhouse with its wealth of architectural detail and store of worldly treasures all to himself. So he opened as a bed and breakfast with four guest rooms just seven years ago.

The inn is filled with fine antiques including a cherry highboy, Early American gaming table, and pencil-post four-poster; herb and flower gardens abound. The innkeeper's prize chickens provide fresh eggs for the morning meal, which also features apple cider from the oldest continuously operated cider mill (just down the road) and toast or muffins with homemade jam.

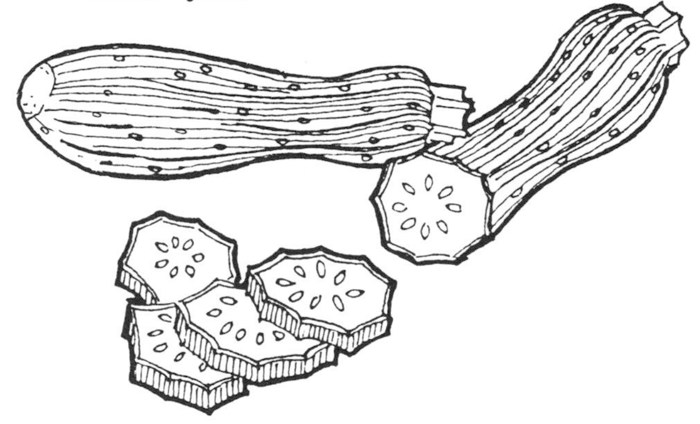

ZUCCHINI MARMALADE

Makes six eight-ounce jars

6 cups peeled and thinly sliced zucchini (about 2 pounds)
Juice of 2 lemons
1 teaspoon grated lemon peel
1-1/2 cups drained, crushed pineapple
One 1-3/4-ounce package powdered fruit pectin
5 cups sugar
2 tablespoons finely chopped crystallized ginger

Place the sliced zucchini in a large kettle. Stir in lemon juice, grated lemon peel, and crushed pineapple. Bring to a boil; lower heat and simmer, uncovered, until the zucchini is tender but still holds its shape (about 15 minutes).

Add fruit pectin and mix well. Turn heat to high and bring to a boil. Stir in sugar and ginger. Bring to a full, rolling boil and boil hard for 1 minute, stirring constantly. Remove from heat; skim off any foam. Stir and skim for 5 minutes to cool and prevent zucchini from floating to the top.

Ladle into 6 hot sterilized 8-ounce jars. Seal according to directions for Preserving Techniques, page 124. Let sit without disturbing for 3–4 hours, check seal, then refrigerate or store in a cool, dark place.

Captain Jefferds Inn

Kennebunkport, Maine

Once the home of an affluent merchant sea captain, this nearly two-hundred-year-old Federal mansion is now the Captain Jefferds Inn. As described by Doug Stewart in *New England's Coastal Journal,* the inn is filled with ". . . enough painstakingly chosen Americana to stock a medium-sized museum." But there is a happy combination of old and new. From wall coverings and window fabrics to bed linens, guest rooms are decorated with Laura Ashley prints, and appointed with maple, pine, and wicker furniture.

Owners, Warren Fitzsimmons and Don Kelly operated a flourishing antique business before purchasing the home. Their good taste and attention to detail are reflected in the inn's warm ambience.

Guests breakfast in the formal dining room, surrounded by fine crystal and china. Summoned to the table by waltz music, everyone is introduced all around before dining on such delights as eggs Benedict, blueberry crêpes, the house "Freak-tata" or ham-and-egg quiche.

FREAK-TATA

Serves four

1/8 cup vegetable oil
1/3 cup diced summer squash
2/3 cup diced zucchini
2/3 cup diced red bell pepper
2/3 cup diced onion
1/4 pound mushrooms, sliced
Salt
Pepper
8 eggs
1/2 cup milk
1-1/2 teaspoons dried sweet basil
3/4 cup grated Parmesan cheese

Preheat oven to 350° F. Heat vegetable oil in a large skillet. Add squash, zucchini, red pepper, and onion; sauté until almost tender. Add mushrooms and sauté for another minute or two. Salt and pepper to taste. Transfer vegetables to a well-buttered 8x8-inch baking dish. Whisk eggs and milk together in a small mixing bowl. Stir in basil. Pour egg mixture over vegetables. Bake 30 minutes. Remove from oven and top with Parmesan cheese. Return to oven for 5–6 minutes to melt the cheese. Serve with hot Italian bread.

BLUEBERRY CREPES

Serves six

CREPES
Makes eighteen four-inch crêpes
3 eggs
1/8 teaspoon salt
1-1/2 cups all-purpose flour
1-1/2 cups milk
2 tablespoons vegetable oil

FILLING
16 ounces blueberries (fresh, canned, or frozen)
2 large ripe bananas, chopped
1-1/2 cups maple syrup

Powdered sugar
Orange slices

CREPES Whisk together eggs and salt in a medium-size mixing bowl. Add flour slowly, alternating with milk. Beat until smooth with a wire whisk or electric mixer. Add oil; stir to blend. Batter should be the consistency of light cream; if too thick, add 2–3 tablespoons more milk. Ladle 3–4 tablespoons of crêpe batter onto a hot lightly oiled griddle, skillet or crêpe pan. Lift and tilt to form crêpe. Cook on both sides until lightly browned. Repeat to make 18 crêpes. Stack and set aside.

FILLING In a medium-size saucepan combine blueberries, bananas and maple syrup. Warm gently over medium low heat.

ASSEMBLY Arrange three crêpes on each plate, unfolded, in a circle. Spoon 1/2 cup of warm blueberry syrup mixture over crêpes. Sprinkle with powdered sugar and garnish with an orange twist.

HAM AND EGG QUICHE

Serves six to eight

PASTRY
1 cup all-purpose flour
1/4 teaspoon salt
6 tablespoons cold butter
1 egg yolk
2 tablespoons water

FILLING
4 eggs
2 cups light cream
1/2 teaspoon salt
1/8 teaspoon ground nutmeg
1 cup diced cooked ham
1 cup grated Swiss cheese

Paprika

PASTRY Combine flour and salt in a bowl. Cut in small chunks of the cold butter with a knife and fork or a pastry blender until the mixture resembles coarse meal. In a small bowl, whisk together egg yolk and water. Add to the flour mixture and blend until pastry holds together in a ball. Wrap in foil; refrigerate 20 minutes. Meanwhile, preheat oven to 425° F. Roll dough out on a floured board to fit a 9-inch pie pan. Transfer dough to pan and press in the bottom and sides of pan. Flute edges. Prick bottom with a fork. Bake (unfilled) for 12 minutes. Let cool.

FILLING Whisk together eggs, cream, salt, and nutmeg in a small mixing bowl. Set aside.

ASSEMBLY Distribute ham over the bottom of the baked pie shell. Spread cheese over the ham. Ladle custard filling over all. Sprinkle with paprika. Bake 15 minutes; lower heat to 350° F and bake for an additional 30 minutes, until a knife inserted in the center comes out clean. Allow to cool 10 minutes. Slice in wedges and serve warm.

Hawthorne Inn

Concord, Massachusetts

Nathaniel Hawthorne loved this land. But then so did Ralph Waldo Emerson, the Alcotts, and Henry David Thoreau. And though Hawthorne Inn proprietor Gregory Burch doesn't want to drop any names, you can bet that on any given evening you might find yourself sharing accommodations here with modern-day luminaries like . . . well, perhaps you should go see for yourself.

Located in the historic zone of Concord, on the famed "Battle Road" of 1775, the Hawthorne Inn is a six-guest-room Colonial appointed with antique furnishings, handmade quilts, Oriental and rag rugs, and original works of art—both ancient and contemporary.

Nathaniel Hawthorne's home, the Wayside, is just across the street. Also located nearby is Emerson's home, the Old Manse, Grapevine Cottage (where the Concord grape was developed), Walden Pond, and the Old North Bridge where the "shot heard 'round the world" was fired.

BREAKFAST AT
THE HAWTHORNE INN

Concord Grape Juice

Fresh Melon Slices

Morning Cake Delight
with
Hawthorne Inn Topping

Brown Breakfast Bread

Fresh Roasted Coffee

MORNING CAKE DELIGHT

Makes one cake

1 pound butter at room temperature
6 eggs
1/2 cup sour cream
1/2 cup milk
1-1/2 teaspoons almond extract
1 tablespoon baking powder
2 cups sugar
1 banana, mashed
4 cups all-purpose flour
1 cup fresh raspberries, blueberries, or blackberries

Preheat oven to 375° F. Mix butter, eggs, sour cream, milk, almond extract, baking powder, sugar, and banana until smooth consistency is reached. Add flour and beat until well mixed; do not overbeat. Pour half of the mixture into a buttered and floured Bundt pan. Add a layer of berries and cover with remaining cake batter. Bake for 1-1/4 hours. Remove from oven, cool, and serve with Hawthorne Inn Topping.

HAWTHORNE INN TOPPING

1/2 cup sour cream
1/2 cup fruit-flavored yogurt
1/2 cup whipping cream

Mix together yogurt and sour cream. Then whip cream and fold in.

BROWN BREAKFAST BREAD

Makes two loaves

3/4 cup honey
3/4 cup molasses
3-1/2 cups whole-wheat flour
2 teaspoons baking soda
2 teaspoons ground ginger
2 teaspoons ground cinnamon
2 teaspoons ground allspice
Dash salt
2 cups milk
1 cup raisins
2 tablespoons orange marmalade

Preheat oven to 350° F. Stir honey and molasses together in a large bowl. Add flour, baking soda, spices, milk, and raisins. Mix well. Stir in orange marmalade. Divide mixture between 2 buttered or oiled 9x5-inch loaf pans and bake 50–60 minutes.

Holiday Inn

Intervale, New Hampshire

Holiday Inn has been operated continuously as an inn since it was built in the late 1800s. But it wasn't until 1984 that Lynne Clough and husband Jim arrived on the scene as the newest innkeepers in the building's lengthy history.

The Cloughs furnished the eleven guest rooms with country antiques, braided rugs, kerosene lamps, and stenciled baskets. There's a fireplace in the homey living room; a swimming pool on the premises.

The inn is located on a peaceful country road surrounded by twenty-five acres of woodland and mountains. Swimming and hiking comprise the summertime activities here; skiing is big in winter and fall foliage is a must.

HOLIDAY INN'S
BUCCANEER BREAKFAST

Chilled Juices

Barbados Fruit Medley

Rum-Runner French Toast

Crisp Bacon and Spicy Sausage

Oatmeal

Mulled Buttery Cider

BARBADOS FRUIT MEDLEY

Serves six
6 bananas
One 20-ounce can pineapple chunks
1/3 cup butter, melted
1/4 teaspoon mace
1/4 teaspoon ground cinnamon
3/4 cup firmly packed brown sugar
1/4 cup raisins
1/2 cup chopped walnuts

Preheat oven to 425° F. Peel bananas, slice lengthwise, and place them in a greased 9x13-inch baking dish. Drain pineapple chunks and arrange over bananas. Combine remaining ingredients; mix and spoon over banana/pineapple mix. Bake 15 minutes. Serve warm.

RUM-RUNNER FRENCH TOAST

Serves six
6 eggs
1-1/2 cups half-and-half
3/4 cup heavy cream
3/4 cup dark rum
3 tablespoons sugar
1-1/2 teaspoons grated orange peel
3 teaspoons vanilla extract
1/4 teaspoon ground cinnamon
1/4 teaspoon ground nutmeg
1/4 pound butter
12 slices raisin bread

Beat eggs, then mix in half-and-half, cream, rum, sugar, orange peel, vanilla, cinnamon, and nutmeg. Heat one-third of the butter in a skillet. Dip raisin bread slices in batter, one at a time, until soaked. Fry 4 slices at a time until golden brown on each side. Remove to a platter and keep warm. Add more butter to skillet and repeat process until all the bread is fried. Serve with maple syrup.

MULLED BUTTERY CIDER

Serves six
1/2 cup brown sugar
Juice from 1 orange
Juice from 1 lemon
1/2 gallon apple cider
4 whole cloves
2 cinnamon sticks
1 teaspoon whole allspice
3 tablespoons butter

In a large saucepan heat sugar and juices until syrupy. Add cider, cloves, cinnamon sticks, and allspice; simmer covered for 1 hour. Strain to remove spices. Pour into mugs and float 1/2 tablespoon butter on top of each.

Waybury Inn

East Middlebury, Vermont

This fine 1810 establishment—built as a stagecoach stop called the Glen House—once provided rooms for women who worked in the local glass factory. It also had its own ballroom for community entertainment. (Makes you wonder how those weary ladies ever got a good night's sleep!)

But there's no question about the quiet surroundings and delightful atmosphere of Waybury Inn today. Its fireside sitting room, full-license pub, art gallery and twelve guest rooms carry on the charm of the building's Colonial heritage in an efficient, modern manner.

Twelve guest rooms? Yes, the choice of accommodations is a rich one. There are king-sized beds, twin beds, and double beds; there are private baths and hall baths. All rooms are furnished with individual appointments that reflect the fine taste of owners Jim and Betty Riley.

Breakfasts are set up buffet style, and on an average morning you might find a variety of homemade muffins, fresh fruit cups, cereals, quiche, and blueberry griddlecakes with, of course, plenty of Vermont maple syrup.

BEST GRIDDLECAKES EVER

Makes ten six-inch griddlecakes
1-3/4 cups all-purpose flour
1/4 cup sugar
2 tablespoons baking powder
4 tablespoons butter, melted
1 egg
1-1/2 cups milk
1/2 cup blueberries
1/2 cup thinly sliced peaches
1/2 cup chopped apples
1/2 cup sliced bananas
Maple syrup

Combine flour, sugar, and baking powder. Stir in butter, egg, and milk; beat to a smooth consistency. Gently fold in fruit. Pour or ladle 1/3 cup batter onto lightly oiled, medium-hot griddle. Cook until small bubbles cover the surface and batter appears dry. Flip griddlecake over to cook other side. Repeat to make 10 griddlecakes. Serve with maple syrup.

MUFFIN FRITTATAS

Makes ten to twelve egg muffins
1 English muffin
8 eggs
2 tablespoons milk
1 cup grated Cheddar cheese
1-1/4 cups diced ham

Preheat oven to 350° F. Render English muffin into very fine crumbs with a blender or food processor. Beat eggs with a fork. Add milk, breadcrumbs, cheese, and ham. Mix thoroughly. Spoon mixture into greased muffin tins (3/4 full) and bake until plump and firm, 20–25 minutes.

The Governor's Inn

Ludlow, Vermont

The Governor's Inn was built as a family residence by Vermont Governor William Wallace Stickney in 1895. The home's original stained-glass windows, golden oak interiors, and Oriental accents bespeak its late Victorian period.

Innkeepers Charlie and Deedy Marble have furnished the hostelry with American antiques from the period 1895 to 1910. Included is a rare teacup collection, which can be viewed from the dining room.

Paul Newman and Joanne Woodward are numbered among the guests of the inn, as are cast members of *Saturday Night Live,* famous models, and both Metropolitan Opera and soap opera stars.

From being "elbow deep" in sandpaper in August of 1982, the Marbles and their Governor's Inn have achieved national acclaim in just two short years. Their recipes have been featured in both *Gourmet* and *Bon Appetit* magazines. Two of the recipes for which they are noted, Charlie's Famous Rum Raisin French Toast and My Great Aunt Fanny's Date Cake, are submitted here. Incidentally, a picture of Great Aunt Fanny hangs above the sideboard in the inn's dining room.

THE GOVERNOR'S BREAKFAST

Freshly Ground Coffee

My Great Aunt Fanny's Date Cake

Fruit Juice

Oatmeal with Raisins

Charlie's Famous Rum Raisin French Toast with Pure Vermont Maple Syrup

MY GREAT AUNT FANNY'S DATE CAKE

Makes one cake

1 cup chopped dates
2-1/2 tablespoons shortening
1 teaspoon baking soda
1 cup boiling water
1 egg, lightly beaten
3/4 cup sugar
1-3/4 cups all-purpose flour
1 teaspoon salt
1 teaspoon vanilla extract
1/2 cup chopped walnuts

Preheat oven to 350° F. To dates add shortening and baking soda. Pour boiling water over mixture. Add egg and sugar; mix well. Stir in flour and salt. Add vanilla and nut meats. Mix all ingredients thoroughly. Pour batter into greased 9x5-inch loaf pan. Bake 55–60 minutes.

CHARLIE'S FAMOUS RUM RAISIN FRENCH TOAST

Serves four

3/4 cup melted rum raisin ice cream
3 eggs, beaten
1 tablespoon dark rum
1/4 teaspoon ground cinnamon
5 tablespoons finely ground walnuts
8 slices raisin bread
Butter
4 scoops rum raisin ice cream
Vermont maple syrup

Combine melted ice cream, eggs, rum, cinnamon, and nuts in a bowl. Beat with a wire whisk until thoroughly blended. Dip raisin bread into egg mixture, coating well on both sides. Sauté in butter over medium heat until toasted. For each serving arrange 2 slices on a warm plate. Top with a small scoop of ice cream and Vermont maple syrup.

The Inn at Manchester

Manchester, Vermont

Built in the late 1800s, the Inn at Manchester has served as a summer vacation home, a full-time family residence, and a ski lodge—the first to open in the area. Today it is a bed and breakfast inn, owned and operated by Stan and Harriet Rosenberg, who took over in 1978.

The setting is as picturebook New England as any you might hope to find, with mountains providing the backdrop and source of winter activities as well.

Victorian antiques dominate the inn's fifteen guest rooms, which also feature posters and paintings, and fluffy comforters on the beds.

Harriet is noted for her country inn cookery, which has been written up in *Travel & Leisure* magazine and *The New York Times.* Here she parts with a family favorite, Peanut Butter Granola. As one enthusiastic guest commented: "Four skis for the food."

HONEY CREAM FRUIT SAUCE

Makes three cups
1 pint sour cream
1/2 cup honey
1/4 cup orange juice

Mix all ingredients thoroughly. Chill. Serve over fresh fruit in season.

PEANUT BUTTER GRANOLA

Makes five cups granola
2-3/4 cups rolled oats
1/4 cup natural wheat germ
1/4 cup sunflower seeds
2 tablespoons vegetable oil
1/3 cup honey
1/3 cup chunky peanut butter
1/4 teaspoon vanilla extract
1/2 cup raisins
1/2 cup chopped walnuts

Preheat oven to 300° F. Stir together oats, wheat germ, and sunflower seeds in a large mixing bowl. In a saucepan heat oil and honey, stirring occasionally. Remove from heat; add peanut butter and vanilla. Pour over dry ingredients and mix well. Spread over a cookie sheet. Bake 20–25 minutes, stirring every 5 minutes so the granola browns evenly. Remove from oven and cool thoroughly. Mix in raisins and nuts. Store in an airtight container.

The Inn at Weston

Weston, Vermont

Take one nineteenth-century farmhouse in the Green Mountains of southern Vermont. Add two friendly people with a genuine interest in others. Stir in a generous dose of publicity and the love of good food. Bake ten years. Now savor the results: The Inn at Weston, home of bed and breakfast innkeepers Sue and Stu Douglas.

This inn rates *Los Angeles Times* Travel Editor Jerry Hulse's "five stars." It hasn't missed the notice of *The New York Times* or *Gourmet* magazine either. And with its eleven antique-filled guest rooms and creative country cuisine, I ask you: What more could a tired and hungry traveler want? Oh, yes—their recipes! Well, here they are.

SUE'S SPECIAL PANCAKES

Makes nine six-inch pancakes

1 cup whole-wheat flour
1/2 cup rye flour
1/2 cup cornmeal
2 teaspoons baking soda
2 eggs
2 cups milk
2 tablespoons sour cream
2 tablespoons butter, melted
Maple syrup

Combine flours, cornmeal, and baking soda. Add eggs, milk, sour cream and butter. Mix well. For each pancake pour or ladle 1/3 cup batter onto a hot greased griddle and cook until small bubbles appear on the surface. Lift and flip pancake(s) over to brown other side. Serve with maple syrup.

BLUEBERRY COFFEECAKE

Makes one large cake

1/2 pound butter, at room temperature
1 cup honey
4 eggs
1 pint sour cream
2 cups whole-wheat flour
2 cups unbleached flour
2 teaspoons baking soda
2 teaspoons baking powder
2 teaspoons vanilla extract
1-1/2 cups blueberries
1/2 cup sugar, mixed with
  2 tablespoons ground cinnamon

Preheat oven to 350° F. Cream soft butter. Stir in honey, eggs, and sour cream. Sift in flours, baking soda, and baking powder. Add vanilla and mix well. Pour half the batter into a greased and floured 9-inch Bundt pan. Cover with a layer of blueberries mixed with half the sugar/cinnamon mix. Pour in remaining batter. Top with remaining sugar/cinnamon. Bake 50–60 minutes.

VERMONT APPLE BUTTER

Makes four pints
5 pounds apples
2 cups apple cider
1 cup sugar
3 teaspoons ground cinnamon
1-1/2 teaspoons ground cloves
1/4 teaspoon ground allspice
Dash ground nutmeg

Wash, stem and core apples. Peel and cut into 1/4-inch wedges. Combine cider and sugar in a 4-1/2-quart kettle. Add apples. Bring to a boil, cover, reduce heat and simmer for 30–40 minutes. Season with cinnamon, cloves, allspice and nutmeg. Continue cooking until apples are soft but still hold their shape a bit (another 5-10 minutes). For smoother consistency whirl through a food processor or press through a sieve before returning to heat. Pack in 4 sterilized 1-pint jars, seal, and process in a water bath for 10 minutes. (See directions for Preserving Techniques, page 124.) Store up to 1 year.

THE MID-ATLANTIC

Alexander's Inn
Barnard-Good House
Captain Mey's
The Mainstay
The Queen Victoria
Summer Cottage Inn
The Wedgwood Inn

Alexander's Inn

Cape May, New Jersey

Alexander's Inn was formerly known as the Joseph Henry Hughes home; the Hughes family being wealthy landowners in Cape May around the turn of the century. Built in 1883, this three-story, twenty-three room mansion is (architecturally speaking) French Revival with its mansard roof and elaborately carved front porch.

Authentic Victorian antiques grace the parlor, the library, the music room and the guest rooms, which are named and decorated by color—Rose Room, Green Room, Silver and Bronze rooms.

Diane Muentz is the chef-in-residence innkeeper. Her husband Larry, a former sales executive with Xerox Corporation, refers to himself as the "nuts and bolts" of the operation. And, if you're wondering about the cuisine, just ask Larry. He'll tell you that even though there are fifty restaurants in Cape May, there's only one Alexander's. In case you think his opinion is biased, consult Chef Tell, who not only stayed here, but sent his compliments to the chef.

ALEXANDER'S INN SUNDAY BRUNCH

Freshly Squeezed Orange Juice

New Jersey Grown Canteloupe and Blackberries

Cassata Toast
with Maple-Honey-Rum Syrup

Fresh Brewed Coffee

CASSATA TOAST

Serves four

FILLING
1/4 cup raisins
1/4 cup dark rum
3/4 cup water
12 ounces ricotta cheese
4 ounces mozzarella cheese, grated

2 loaves Italian bread, or
 1 large loaf French bread

BATTER
2 eggs, beaten
2 cups light cream or half-and-half
3 tablespoons Grand Marnier
Sprinkling of ground nutmeg

Maple-Honey-Rum Syrup, following

Add raisins to rum and water; soak in refrigerator overnight. Drain raisins and mix with cheeses. To assemble, slice bread in 1-inch diagonal slices. Slit each slice lengthwise through center of crust almost all the way down through dough to form a "pocket." Using your hands, press as much of the filling into each pocketed slice of bread as it will hold (as much as 4 tablespoons). Clean the excess off the outside; it will burn if it touches the griddle. (The bread may be stuffed hours in advance and refrigerated.)

Mix batter ingredients together. Dip each slice of filled bread into batter and turn to coat evenly. Fry on lightly oiled (not buttered) griddle, browning each side slowly over medium heat. Keep warm until all slices are done. Serve with warmed Maple-Honey-Rum Syrup.

MAPLE-HONEY-RUM SYRUP

Makes two cups
1 cup pure Vermont maple syrup
1 cup honey
2 tablespoons dark rum, or
 1 tablespoon rum flavoring
1 tablespoon vanilla extract

Mix all ingredients and stir over low heat until warm and completely blended. Can be stored, covered, in the refrigerator for several weeks.

Barnard-Good House

Cape May, New Jersey

In February of 1980 Nan and Tom Hawkins fell in love with this 1865 Second Empire Victorian with mansard roof, full wraparound veranda, and abundance of ornamental gingerbread trim. By the Fourth of July they were moved in and in business—the bed and breakfast business—with accommodations for twelve.

The inn's guest rooms, furnished with antiques of the period, feature canopy and brass beds. The living room has a century-old pump organ; the dining room a gasolier of pewter, brass, and iron.

Hallmark of the Barnard-Good House is its breakfast (both delicious and unique) often including soup, cake, and meat-filled crêpes. As New Jersey is known as the "Garden State," Nan tries to incorporate as much of the local bounty as possible into the morning menu. Fruit dishes concur with the season.

BRUNCH AT BARNARD-GOOD HOUSE

Fresh Peach Soup

Chicken Crab Crêpes

Crumb Swirl Coffeecake

Buns of Gold

Fresh Pear Cranberry Butter Crunch

Viennese Roast Coffee

FRESH PEACH SOUP

Serves four to six

5 large ripe peaches, peeled and quartered
1/4 cup sugar
1 cup plain yogurt
1/4 cup fresh orange juice
1/4 cup fresh lemon juice
1/4 cup cream sherry
Fresh mint

Purée peaches with sugar in food processor or blender. Blend in yogurt. Add orange and lemon juices. Add sherry and mix until smooth. Pour into bowl, cover, and refrigerate overnight. Garnish with fresh mint.

CRUMB SWIRL COFFEECAKE

Makes two coffeecakes

4 cups all-purpose flour
1/4 teaspoon salt
One 1/4-ounce package active dry yeast
1/4 pound butter
3 eggs
1/4 cup sugar
1 cup lukewarm water
1 cup very fine vanilla wafer crumbs
2 cups packed light brown sugar
3/4 cup chopped pecans
Powdered sugar

In food processor bowl (or large mixing bowl), stir together flour, salt, and yeast. Add butter and process (or use a pastry blender) until particles are size of peas. In a mixing bowl beat eggs with a fork or wire whisk. Add sugar and water, then flour mixture. Mix well and form into a dough. Cover and chill at least 3 hours, preferably overnight. Divide dough in half and turn out on floured board. Roll each piece out to a 20x14-inch rectangle. Mix together wafer crumbs, brown sugar and pecans and sprinkle half the mixture over each piece of dough. Roll each into a tight roll, seal and shape into a ring with seam side down. Let rise in warm area for 1 hour. Bake in preheated 375° F. oven 25–30 minutes, until brown. Dust with powdered sugar.

CHICKEN CRAB CREPES

Serves six

CREPE BATTER
2 eggs
1/8 teaspoon salt
1 cup milk
1 cup all-purpose flour
4 tablespoons butter, melted

FILLING
5 tablespoons unsalted butter
5–6 shallots, peeled and thinly sliced
1/4 pound fresh mushrooms, sliced
3 tablespoons all-purpose flour
1 cup chicken broth
1/4 cup light cream
1/4 cup dry white wine
1 cup cooked, shredded chicken breast
1 cup cooked, shredded crabmeat
1/2 cup grated Parmesan cheese
1/4 teaspoon dried rosemary
1/2 teaspoon salt
1 cup grated Swiss cheese
Parsley sprigs

CREPES Combine all ingredients in blender jar; blend for about 1 minute. Scrape down sides and blend another 15 seconds, until smooth. Refrigerate at least 1 hour. Heat a lightly oiled griddle, skillet or crêpe pan. Pour or spoon 3–4 tablespoons of batter in pan and spread out to form a round, 6-inch crêpe. Brown lightly on one side only. Stack crêpes between layers of waxed paper and set aside. (Makes 12–15 crêpes.)

FILLING Melt 2 tablespoons butter in a large saucepan. Add shallots and mushrooms; sauté until limp. Stir in remaining butter until melted. Add flour; cook and stir until bubbly. Gradually stir in broth, cream, and wine; remove from heat. Add chicken, crabmeat, Parmesan, rosemary, and salt and mix well.

ASSEMBLY Preheat oven to 400° F. Fill crêpes and roll, placing them seam side down in a buttered 9x13-inch baking dish. Top with Swiss cheese and bake 20–30 minutes. Garnish with parsley.

BUNS OF GOLD

Makes two dozen buns

1 cup water
1/4 pound butter
1 teaspoon sugar
1/4 teaspoon salt
1 cup all-purpose flour
4 eggs
1/2 cup raisins, plumped in
 1-1/2 cups boiling water

FROSTING
1 tablespoon butter
1-1/2 tablespoons heavy cream
3/4 cup powdered sugar
1 teaspoon vanilla extract

BUNS Preheat oven to 375° F. Combine water, butter, sugar, and salt in saucepan. Bring to a boil. Add flour all at once, lower heat, and beat until mixture leaves sides of pan. Remove from heat and stir until slightly cool. Add eggs, one at a time, beating well after each. Drain raisins and stir in. Drop batter by tablespoons onto a greased cookie sheet, about 1 inch apart. Bake 30 minutes. Cool.

FROSTING Melt butter, stir in cream and remove from heat. Stir in powdered sugar and vanilla. Frost cooled buns.

FRESH PEAR AND CRANBERRY BUTTER CRUNCH

Serves eight to ten

4 ripe pears, peeled, cored, and sliced
One 12-ounce bag fresh cranberries
1/3 cup sugar
1 teaspoon ground cinnamon
3 tablespoons all-purpose flour
2/3 cup firmly packed brown sugar
3/4 cup rolled oats
1/2 cup all-purpose flour
1/4 pound butter

Preheat oven to 375° F. Combine pear slices, cranberries, sugar, cinnamon, and 3 tablespoons flour. Place in buttered 9x13-inch baking dish. In a mixing bowl combine brown sugar, oats, and 1/2 cup flour. Cut butter into small pieces and cut into oats mixture with a knife and fork or pastry cutter. Sprinkle over pear/cranberry mixture. Bake 45 minutes. Cut into squares before serving.

Captain Mey's

Cape May, New Jersey

Captain Mey's namesake is one Cornelius J. Mey, who was sent by the Dutch West India Company in a vessel named *Good Tidings* to explore North America's coast in 1621. In keeping with the namesake's heritage—as well as that of the innkeepers—a Dutch theme prevails. A delft ware collection and Dutch artifacts are found throughout the inn; the spacious guest rooms also incorporate antique walnut beds, marble-topped dressers, handmade quilts, and fresh flowers.

A typical Dutch breakfast is served by candlelight; classical music can be heard playing in the background. Included among the offerings are cheeses imported from Holland, homemade yogurt, and freshly baked breads.

CAPTAIN MEY'S
DUTCH INN BREAKFAST

Homemade Vanilla Honey Yogurt

Dutch Apple Cake

Edam and Gouda Cheeses
Served with Breakfast Meats

Cobblestone Bread

Dutch Chocolate Coffee

COBBLESTONE BREAD

Makes one loaf

4 teaspoons active dry yeast
1/2 cup lukewarm water
1 teaspoon maple syrup
3-1/4 cups whole-wheat flour
1 teaspoon sea salt
3 eggs
1/4 cup corn oil
Sesame seeds

Bring all ingredients (except water) to room temperature. Dissolve yeast in water. Add syrup and mix well. Set aside. Sift flour and salt into a large mixing bowl. Separate into two bowls the white from the yolk of 1 egg. Add the remaining eggs and corn oil to the egg white. Beat well; add to yeast mixture. Add half the flour to the liquid and mix well. Add remaining flour, mixing to blend. Knead dough on lightly floured board for approximately 10 minutes, until dough is soft and pliable. Form the dough into a ball and place in an oiled bowl. Turn dough to coat with oil. Cover bowl with a plate and let rise in a warm place for 50–60 minutes, until double. Punch down and let rise again for 30–40 minutes.

Punch down and divide into 3 equal pieces. Roll each into a ball, then into 12-inch-long strands. Sprinkle the strands with flour and braid them together, tucking the ends under neatly. Place on an oiled baking sheet. Add 1 teaspoon of water to the reserved egg yolk, mix, and brush on the top of the loaf. Sprinkle on sesame seeds. Cover and let rise in a warm place 45–55 minutes. Preheat oven to 375° F. Bake 30–35 minutes.

DUTCH APPLE CAKE

Makes one large cake

3 cups all-purpose flour
3 teaspoons baking powder
2 cups sugar
1 cup vegetable oil
5 eggs
1/4 cup orange juice
2-1/2 teaspoons vanilla extract
5 medium apples, peeled, cored, and sliced
2 teaspoons ground cinnamon, mixed with
  5 tablespoons sugar

Preheat oven to 350° F. Combine flour, baking powder, sugar, vegetable oil, eggs, orange juice, and vanilla; mix well. Pour a fourth of the batter into a well-greased and floured 9x13-inch cake pan. Arrange half of the apple slices on top and sprinkle with half of the cinnamon/sugar mixture. Pour remaining batter into pan. Arrange remaining apple slices on top; sprinkle with the rest of the cinnamon/sugar mixture. Bake 1-1/2 hours.

The Mainstay

Cape May, New Jersey

In 1872 two wealthy gamblers pooled their resources to build an elaborate clubhouse where they and their friends could pursue their gentlemanly interests. No expense was spared, and the result—a grand villa with fourteen-foot ceilings, chandeliers, a sweeping veranda, and an ornate cupola—was the talk of the town. This "clubhouse" still causes a stir, but today it attracts guests (not gamblers) and is fondly known as The Mainstay bed and breakfast inn.

The twelve-guest-room mansion encompasses the treasures and traditions of its time. It is furnished with Victorian antiques (many of which are original to the house). The coal-burning stove still warms the parlor. And guests, like their ancestors, can enjoy a game of croquet on the lawn, a hand of cards in the drawing room, and an ample breakfast on the veranda.

Proprietors Tom and Sue Carroll (who have produced an informal cookbook of their own that has already sold well over five thousand copies) have agreed to share two of their most popular recipes.

MAINSTAY INN BREAKFAST

Fresh Fruit Juice

Virginia Ham and Apple Pie

Cheddar Cheese Muffins

Coffee and Tea

VIRGINIA HAM AND APPLE PIE

Serves six

3 tablespoons all-purpose flour
3/4 cup firmly packed brown sugar
1/2 teaspoon ground cinnamon
1/4 teaspoon mace
A few grinds fresh black pepper
5 medium apples, peeled, cored, and sliced
1-1/2 cups diced cooked ham

PIE CRUST
1 cup all-purpose flour
1/4 teaspoon salt
4 tablespoons butter, cut into small chunks
3 tablespoons cold water

6 slices Edam cheese

Preheat oven to 350° F. Combine flour, brown sugar, cinnamon, mace, and black pepper. Set aside. Grease a 7x10-inch baking dish. Layer a third of the apples with half of the ham in the bottom of the dish. Sprinkle with half of the seasonings. Layer another third of the apples and the remaining ham and seasonings. Top with remaining apples. Set aside.

To make pie crust, combine flour and salt. Cut in butter with a pastry blender. Add water, a little at a time, to form dough into a ball. Roll out on a floured board to a 7-1/2x10-1/2-inch rectangle.

Cover apples with the pie crust dough, sealing the edges. Bake for 1 hour. Remove from oven and cut into 6 squares. Top each with a thin slice of Edam cheese. Return to oven until cheese is melted. Serve immediately.

CHEDDAR CHEESE MUFFINS

Makes fifteen muffins

2 cups all-purpose flour
3 teaspoons baking powder
1 tablespoon sugar
1/2 teaspoon salt
1 egg
1 cup milk
3 tablespoons butter, softened
1-1/2 cups grated sharp Cheddar cheese

Preheat oven to 400° F. Mix flour, baking powder, sugar, and salt in medium-size bowl. Set aside. Put egg, milk, and butter into blender or food processor bowl; cover and whirl until smooth. Stir in grated cheese. Pour wet ingredients into dry and mix until just moistened. Spoon into greased and floured muffin tins (3/4 full) and bake for 20–25 minutes.

The Queen Victoria

Cape May, New Jersey

This dark green Italianate Victorian with its wine-red trim was built by Delaware River pilot Douglas Gregory in 1881. Nearly a century later the property was acquired by Joan and Dane Wells (a former executive director for the Victorian Society of America and a participant in Philadelphia's commercial neighborhood revitalization program, respectively). They wedded their expertise to restore the twenty-eight-room mansion, turning it into a bed and breakfast venture recognized far beyond the boundaries of Cape May—a town designated National Historic Landmark status by the U.S. Department of Interior.

Much of the Queen's appeal is accredited to her abundance of epicurean delights: A fruit basket awaits guests of the inn, tea and cookies are served around five, a piece of fresh fudge sits on the bed pillow, and the breakfast buffet on the sideboard promises a great day ahead. Nothing is leftover, according to Joan, much to the dismay of the three cats in residence: Mumbles, Sketty, and Snowshoes—the "king" of the Queen Victoria.

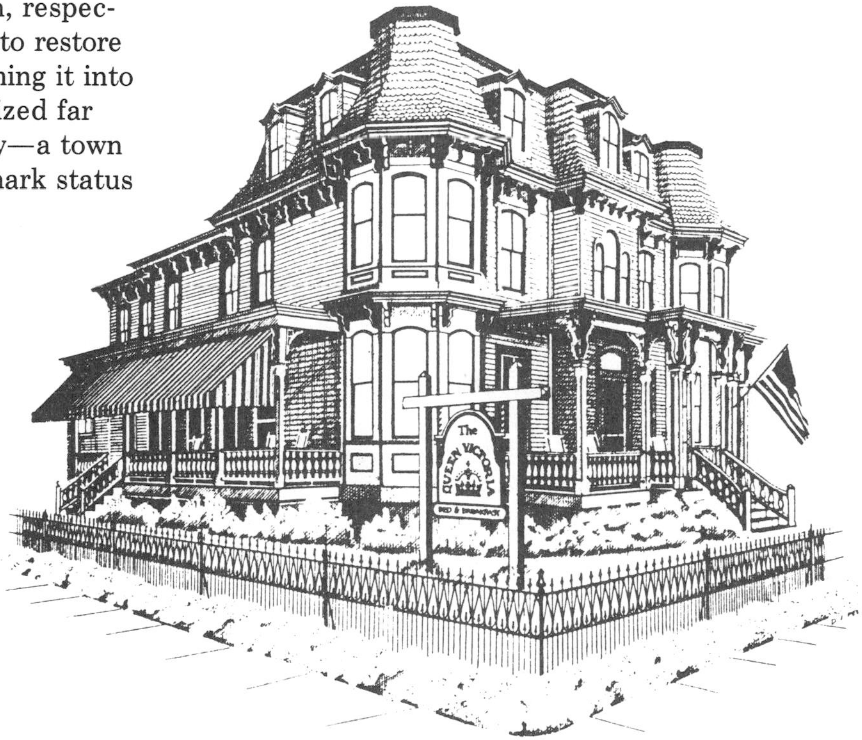

A BOUNTEOUS BREAKFAST AT THE QUEEN VICTORIA

Fresh Jersey Fruits in Season

Eggs Florentine
with Sautéeed Cherry Tomatoes

Chocolate Yogurt Cake

The Queen's Oats

Whole-Wheat Rolls
with Rhubarb Marmalade

Selection of Imported English Teas

The Queen's Own Blend of Coffee

EGGS FLORENTINE

Serves twelve

9 eggs
1 pint creamed cottage cheese
8 ounces Swiss cheese, grated
8 ounces feta cheese, cubed
4 tablespoons butter, softened
Two 10-ounce packages frozen chopped spinach, thawed and well drained
1 teaspoon ground nutmeg

Preheat oven to 350° F. Beat eggs slightly. Add cheeses and butter; mix well. Stir in spinach and nutmeg. Pour into greased 9x13-inch baking dish. Bake 1 hour, until knife inserted in center comes out clean.

THE QUEEN'S OATS

Makes sixteen cups of granola

8 cups rolled oats (not quick or instant)
1-1/2 cups firmly packed brown sugar
1-1/2 cups unprocessed bran
1-1/2 cups natural wheat germ (not toasted or honey)
1/2 cup walnuts
1/2 cup raw sunflower seeds
1/2 cup vegetable oil
3/4 cup honey
2 teaspoons vanilla extract
2 cups raisins

Preheat oven to 325° F. Stir to blend oats, sugar, bran, wheat germ, walnuts, and sunflower seeds. In a small saucepan heat oil, honey, and vanilla over medium flame; stirring until bubbly. Thoroughly mix liquids with dry ingredients. Bake in a large stainless steel bowl or 8-quart kettle, or divide mixture evenly between 2 rimmed baking sheets. Bake 15–20 minutes, stirring every 5 minutes to keep granola evenly browned. Stir again several times as the mixture cools to prevent it from sticking together. When thoroughly cool, add the raisins. Store in an airtight container.

WHOLE-WHEAT ROLLS

Makes one dozen rolls

One 1/4-ounce package active dry yeast
1-1/4 cups warm water
1-1/2 teaspoons salt
1 tablespoon butter, softened
1 tablespoon sugar
1 cup whole-wheat flour
2-1/4 cups all-purpose flour
Cornmeal

Dissolve yeast in warm water; stir in salt, butter, sugar, and whole-wheat flour. Gradually work in all-purpose flour. Knead dough on floured, smooth surface 10 minutes. Place in an oiled bowl, turning to spread oil on top of dough. Cover and let rise in a draft-free, warm place until doubled in size, approximately 40 minutes. Punch down, cover and let rise again until doubled in size, approximately 30 minutes. Punch down, turn onto a floured surface, and divide dough in half. Form each half into a 12-inch-long roll. Cut each roll crosswise into 6 pieces. Place pieces well apart on 2 large cornmeal-sprinkled baking sheets. Cover and let rise 20 minutes. (Rolls lengthen but do not rise too high.) In the meantime, preheat oven to 400° F. Bake rolls until brown and crusty, about 20 minutes.

CHOCOLATE YOGURT CAKE

Makes one large cake

2 cups plus 1 tablespoon all-purpose flour
2/3 cup plus 1 teaspoon processed Dutch cocoa
1-1/2 teaspoons baking soda
1/4 pound butter, softened
1-1/2 cups sugar
2 eggs
1-1/2 cups plain yogurt
1 teaspoon vanilla extract
Powdered sugar

Preheat oven to 350° F. Oil a 9-inch Bundt or tube pan. Mix 1 tablespoon flour with 1 teaspoon cocoa and dust the inside of the pan; shake out any excess. Sift remaining flour and cocoa together with baking soda. Set aside. Cream butter with sugar. Beat in eggs, one at a time. Add flour mixture alternately with yogurt. Do not overmix. Stir in vanilla. Pour batter into prepared pan and bake for 45–55 minutes (until toothpick inserted into center comes out clean). Cool for 10 minutes before inverting onto a cooling rack to release from pan. Cool completely and dust with powdered sugar.

Summer Cottage Inn

Cape May, New Jersey

The Summer Cottage Inn, built in 1867 by the renowned architect Stephen Decatur Button, is Italianate in design. The house was commissioned for a family summer residence by one S.A. Harrison, and remained such through the late 1800s and early 1900s. Since then it has served as a restaurant, and finally a guest house for many years.

Innkeeper Nancy Rishforth names cooking among her list of favorite activities, others of which include conversing with the inn's many delightful guests and imbibing the beautiful surroundings of Cape May, the nation's oldest seaside resort.

The inn's guest rooms (furnished with country Victorian, wicker and nostalgia pieces) provide a restful retreat, the veranda enjoys the cool ocean breeze, and the beach lies just a block away. But the real enjoyment is found at the breakfast table where the Summer Cottage Torte is the main topic of conversation—and the inn's most sought-after recipe as well.

SUMMER COTTAGE SPECIALTIES

Baked Peaches à la Raspberry

Summer Cottage Torte

Rum-Raisin Buns

Juice, Coffee, Tea

BAKED PEACHES A LA RASPBERRY

Serves six

6 medium-size peaches
Raspberry jam*
Heavy cream

Preheat oven to 350° F. Wash peaches and slice a thin piece off the top of each. Remove pit and stuff the cavity with raspberry jam. Place filled peaches into a shallow, greased baking dish. Bake 30–40 minutes. Cool and refrigerate at least 3 hours. Serve chilled in a pool of cream.

**The Summer Cottage Inn uses homemade raspberry jam for this recipe. You can use your favorite store-bought brand, or there's a very good recipe on page 59.*

SUMMER COTTAGE TORTE

Serves six

Eight 8-inch crêpes*
One 10-ounce package frozen chopped spinach, cooked and well drained
1 pound bulk sausage, sautéed and crumbled
6 tablespoons butter
1/4 cup finely chopped onion
4 tablespoons all-purpose flour
Two 13-ounce cans evaporated milk
8 ounces sharp Cheddar cheese, grated**
1/2 teaspoon salt
1/2 teaspoon pepper
1/4 cup finely chopped fresh basil, or 1/2 teaspoon dried basil
Dash ground nutmeg
Cherry tomatoes

Prepare crêpes, spinach, and sausage. Melt butter in a large skillet; add onions and sauté until golden. Sprinkle in flour; cook and stir until bubbly. Slowly add milk, stirring and cooking until very thick. Add cheeses and seasonings; stir until blended. Reserve 1/2 cup of sauce. To remaining sauce mix in spinach and sausage to make the torte filling.

To assemble, place one crêpe on a lightly buttered baking sheet. Spread 3–4 tablespoons of filling over the crêpe, starting from the center. Repeat with layers of crêpes and filling, stacking as you go, ending with a crêpe. Top torte with reserved sauce. Cover and refrigerate overnight. Preheat oven to 375° F. Bake 35 minutes. Remove from oven and allow to settle (4–5 minutes) before transfering to a serving platter. Garnish with cherry tomatoes and cut into wedges to serve.

**There are a number of good crêpe batter recipes in this book; the easiest is from the Romeo Inn, page 114.*

***The innkeeper recommends using 4 ounces of sharp Cheddar cheese and 4 ounces of Kraft Old English cheese.*

RUM-RAISIN BUNS

Makes two dozen buns

1/2 cup golden raisins
1/4 pound butter
1 cup water
1 tablespoon sugar
1 teaspoon salt
1 cup all-purpose flour
4 eggs

FROSTING
2 tablespoons butter
2 tablespoons light cream
1-1/2 cups powdered sugar
1 tablespoon dark rum

Preheat oven to 375° F. Plump raisins in hot water for 5 minutes; drain well. Combine butter, water, sugar, and salt in a saucepan over medium high heat; bring to a boil. Reduce heat to low. Stir in flour and beat with a wooden spoon until mixture forms into a ball. Remove from heat and continue beating 2 minutes more to cool. Add eggs, one at a time, beating mixture after each to maintain a smooth consistency. Stir in raisins. Drop by tablespoons onto a buttered baking sheet. Bake 30 minutes, until golden brown. Cool and frost.

FROSTING Melt butter; remove from heat. Stir in cream and sugar. Beat until smooth. Add rum; stir to blend.

The Wedgwood Inn

New Hope, Pennsylvania

Located just two blocks from the historic district in the heart of New Hope, this two-and-one-half-story Victorian with gabled hip roof and scroll-carved wraparound veranda offers lodging in the classic bed and breakfast tradition.

Proprietors Carl Glassman and Nadine Silnutzer have filled the premise's interiors with nineteenth-century antiques, Wedgwood pottery, original works of art, and handmade quilts. Exteriors reveal a sun porch, gazebo, an abundance of colorful flower beds, and a well-manicured lawn.

One enters the drive on the same road trod by General Alexander Lord Stirling during the Revolutionary War. Today's travelers, however, are pursuing more pleasurable pastimes like swimming and canoeing down the lazy Delaware River and biking along the gently rolling countryside. Bucks County is known as a major crafts and antiques center. The inn is listed on the National Register of Historic Places.

THE WEDGWOOD BREAKFAST BREADS

Irish Soda Bread

English Muffin Bread

Sesame Banana Bread

Sesame Zucchini Bread

IRISH SODA BREAD

Makes one loaf

3 cups all-purpose flour
2 teaspoons baking powder
1/2 teaspoon baking soda
1 teaspoon salt
1/4 cup sugar
1 cup raisins
1 tablespoon caraway seeds
1-1/2 cups buttermilk

Preheat oven to 350° F. Sift together flour, baking powder, soda, salt, and sugar. Stir in raisins and caraway seeds. Pour in buttermilk and mix well. Knead on floured surface 3–5 minutes. Place in oiled and floured 9-inch round cake pan. Bake 1 hour. Remove loaf from pan and cool on a rack.

ENGLISH MUFFIN BREAD

Makes two loaves

3 cups all-purpose flour
Two 1/4-ounce packages active dry yeast
1 tablespoon sugar
2 teaspoons salt
1/4 teaspoon baking soda
2 cups milk
1/2 cup water
2-1/2 additional cups all-purpose flour (approximate)
Cornmeal

Preheat oven to 400° F. Combine 3 cups flour with yeast, sugar, salt, and soda. Set aside. Heat milk and water in a saucepan until lukewarm. Add all at once to dry mixture; beat well. Stir in enough additional flour (up to 2-1/2 cups) to make a stiff dough. Divide between two 9x5-inch loaf pans that have been oiled and sprinkled with cornmeal. Sprinkle tops with cornmeal. Cover and let rise in a warm place for 45 minutes. Bake 25 minutes. Remove from pan immediately. Slice while warm and serve. Or cool on a rack for later use; slices may be toasted before serving.

SESAME BANANA BREAD

Makes one loaf

1/4 pound butter, softened
1/2 cup sugar
2 eggs
3 ripe bananas, mashed
1/4 cup milk
1 teaspoon vanilla extract
2 cups all-purpose flour
1 teaspoon baking soda
1/2 teaspoon salt
1 cup sesame seeds

Preheat oven to 350° F. Cream butter and sugar together until fluffy. Add eggs, one at a time. Stir in bananas, milk, and vanilla. Add remaining ingredients and mix well. Pour into oiled 9x5-inch loaf pan. Bake 50–60 minutes. Remove from pan, slice, and serve while still warm. Or cool on a rack, wrap, and store for future use.

SESAME ZUCCHINI BREAD

Makes two loaves

3 eggs
1 cup sugar
1 cup vegetable oil
2 cups grated zucchini
3 teaspoons vanilla extract
3 cups all-purpose flour
1 teaspoon salt
1 teaspoon baking soda
1-1/2 teaspoons baking powder
3 teaspoons ground cinnamon
1-1/2 cups sesame seeds

Preheat oven to 350° F. Beat eggs until light and foamy. Add sugar, oil, zucchini, and vanilla. Mix lightly, then beat well. Add remaining ingredients and mix well. Divide batter into 2 oiled 9x5-inch loaf pans. Bake 1 hour. Remove from pan, slice and serve while still warm. Or cool on a rack, wrap, and store for later use.

CARL'S CHEESE GRITS A LA NEW HOPE

Serves eight
2 ounces jalapeño cheese
2 ounces Cheddar cheese
2 ounces mozzarella cheese
6 cups boiling water
1-1/2 cups quick grits
4 tablespoons butter
1/2 teaspoon garlic salt
2 tablespoons milk
1 egg
Paprika

Preheat oven to 400° F. Coarsely grate or cube the cheeses. Pour grits, butter, and garlic salt into boiling water. Stir to mix, cover, reduce heat, and simmer for 5 minutes. (Stir occasionally to insure a smooth consistency.) Remove from heat and add milk and egg as well as grated cheeses. Mix until blended and pour into a greased 10x7-inch baking dish. Sprinkle with paprika. Bake 30 minutes.

HOT BUTTERED WEDGWOOD

Serves two
2 ounces almond liqueur
2 cups hot tea, cider, or apple juice
1 tablespoon whipped unsalted butter
2 twists orange peel
2 cinnamon sticks

Pour 1 ounce almond liqueur into each mug. Fill with hot tea, cider, or juice. Top each with 1/2 tablespoon whipped, unsalted butter. Garnish with an orange peel twist and cinnamon stick.

THE SOUTH

Devon Cottage

Eureka Springs, Arkansas

The idea of offering bed and breakfast in her own home occurred to Arkansawyer Laura Menees while she was touring the English countryside. The thought struck her in Devonshire, to be exact. So it naturally followed that once back in the Ozarks Laura would name her newly opened inn Devon Cottage.

The Edwardian-style dwelling sits high on a ridge overlooking charming Eureka Springs. Its spacious rooms are furnished with handsome oak and wicker pieces, colorful quilts, and local folk art. Breakfast is served around a big oak table. It begins with French-roast coffee, followed by fresh juice or fruits of the season and homebaked breads. But that's not all: Ham and asparagus crêpes, mushroom quiche, and oatmeal-black walnut pancakes clinch it for the happy guest.

FRAMBOISE CREAM

Makes one cup syrup
1/2 cup raspberry jam
1/2 cup liqueur de framboise (raspberry liqueur)
Whipped cream

Bring jam and liqueur to a slow simmer. Cool and refrigerate. Stir several tablespoons of syrup into whipped cream as needed and serve over sliced fresh fruit.

BANANA'S AMARETTO

Serves four
2 tablespoons butter
1 tablespoon light brown sugar
6 bananas, sliced
1/4 cup coconut Amaretto
Whipped cream
Ground nutmeg

Melt butter in a skillet. Add brown sugar and sauté bananas until slightly soft, but not mushy. Gently stir in liqueur. Serve in individual ramekins, topped with whipped cream and a sprinkling of nutmeg.

BLUEBERRY BREAD PUDDING

Serves four to six
3 blueberry muffins*
1-1/2 cups milk
2 tablespoons honey
3 eggs, beaten
2 tablespoons butter
1 cup fresh or frozen blueberries
2 tablespoons grated lemon rind

Preheat oven to 350° F. Crumble muffins into a greased 1-quart casserole. Mix milk and honey with beaten eggs; pour over muffins. Dot with butter and top with blueberries. Sprinkle with grated lemon rind. Bake 40 minutes, until set.

**The innkeeper uses homemade blueberry muffins; bakery muffins will work equally well. Or, you can make your own using the recipe on page 98.*

OATMEAL-BLACK WALNUT PANCAKES

Makes sixteen four-inch pancakes
1-1/2 cups uncooked rolled oats
1 cup all-purpose flour
2 tablespoons brown sugar
1/4 teaspoon salt
3 teaspoons baking powder
1/2 cup chopped black walnuts
1-1/2 cups milk
2 eggs
2 tablespoons butter, melted
Orange Sauce, following

Combine oats, flour, brown sugar, salt, baking powder, and black walnuts; set aside. Whisk together milk, eggs, and melted butter. Pour over dry ingredients and mix until just combined. Spoon by quarter cupfuls onto heated, lightly oiled griddle. Cook until bubbles form on the surface and edges become dry. Flip over and cook until golden brown. Serve with Orange Sauce.

ORANGE SAUCE

Makes one cup
3/4 cup brown sugar
4 tablespoons butter
1/2 cup fresh orange juice
1 tablespoon grated orange rind

Combine ingredients in saucepan. Simmer 5 minutes, stirring constantly. Cool slightly and serve over Oatmeal-Black Walnut Pancakes.

EAST INDIAN TEA

Serves four
2 cups milk
2 cups water
2 cinnamon sticks
1 teaspoon whole cloves
1 teaspoon whole coriander
1/2 teaspoon whole cardamom
2 tablespoons orange pekoe tea

Boil all ingredients (except tea) together for 5 minutes. Add tea, cover, and remove from heat. Steep 5 additional minutes. Strain and serve.

PAPAYA SMOOTHY

Serves four
1 large ripe papaya
2 cups milk
1/4 cup Triple Sec
Kiwi or lime slices

Cut papaya in half, remove seeds, and scoop out pulp into a blender. Add milk and Triple Sec; blend until smooth. Serve in chilled glasses garnished with kiwi or lime slices.

The Greystone Inn

Savannah, Georgia

What a setup for a B&B! From its conception this 1858 Federal townhouse of Savannah merchant John Bartow Howell was destined to showcase the graciousness of life among the prominent and wealthy of the Old South.

Today you need to be neither prominent nor wealthy to experience the grandeur that makes itself apparent from the moment you enter the Greystone's foyer.

A mahogany staircase leads to the parlor where period antiques rest on Oriental carpets; crystal chandeliers cast a soft glow on rich tapestries and displayed objects d'art. Seven bedrooms are fitted with English Regency chairs, tilt-top candle stands and eighteenth-century chests of drawers. Such elegance notwithstanding, the dining room is where guests savor the ultimate in Southern hospitality and Southern cuisine.

SHRIMP SAVANNAH

Serves four to six

2 pounds raw shrimp, peeled and deveined
1 small onion, grated
4 lemon slices
1/4 pound butter
1/2 cup all-purpose flour
2 cups half-and-half
2 cups milk
1/4 cup dry white wine
1/2 cup grated mozzarella cheese
2 tablespoons chopped fresh parsley
1/4 cup grated Parmesan cheese
Paprika
4–6 slices of toasted bread, cut diagonally

Preheat oven to 350° F. In a large Dutch oven place shrimp, onion, and lemon slices. Cover with water and bring to a boil. Reduce heat and simmer 3–4 minutes. Drain shrimp and remove lemon slices. In a saucepan melt butter and stir in flour. Slowly add half-and-half and milk, stirring constantly until thick and bubbly. Remove from heat. Mix in white wine, mozzarella, and parsley. Return shrimp to Dutch oven and pour sauce over it. Sprinkle with Parmesan and paprika to taste. Bake 10 minutes. Serve over toast points.

QUICK HOT CINNAMON APPLESAUCE

Serves four to six

One 24-ounce jar (2-3/4 cups) applesauce
1/2 cup firmly packed brown sugar
1/2 cup sugar
2 teaspoons ground cinnamon
Dash ground nutmeg
2 tablespoons butter

Combine and mix all ingredients in a saucepan. Cook over medium heat for 4–5 minutes.

The Burn

Natchez, Mississippi

This three-story Greek mansion, built in 1832, is one of Natchez' most historic plantation homes. Large Doric pilasters support the front portico, priceless antiques fill the guest rooms (Victorian, Federal, and New York Empire pieces are included), and the original dependancy, which formerly housed the plantation school, is once again in use with four guest rooms.

Natchez Mayor Tony Byrne and his restaurateur wife Loretta had restored two other homes in the area prior to purchasing The Burn and turning it into a bed and breakfast inn that plays host to visitors from around the globe.

Plantation home tours provide the area's main attraction, and while a typical plantation breakfast usually consists of buttermilk biscuits, an egg omelette and cheese grits, Loretta has sent along her recipes for what she calls a "Monday Morning Quickie"—a breakfast you can fix in a jiffy.

THE BURN'S MONDAY MORNING QUICKIE

Muffin Yummies

Soft Scrambled Eggs with Sour Cream and Chopped Chives

Hot Amaretto Fruit

Orange Juice

Hot Coffee

MUFFIN YUMMIES

Serves six

1/2 pound bulk sausage
1 small onion, chopped
One 5-ounce jar Kraft Old English Cheddar Cheese Spread
1/4 pound butter
1/4 teaspoon garlic salt
1 tablespoon Worcestershire sauce
6 English muffins, sliced

Preheat oven to 350° F. Crumble and brown sausage in skillet. Add onion and sauté until limp; drain well. Add remaining ingredients and mix well. Remove from heat and cool slightly. Spoon on sliced muffins and bake 10 minutes. May be made ahead of time and refrigerated until time to bake and serve.

HOT AMARETTO FRUIT

Serves six
Two 30-ounce cans fruit cocktail*
1 cup pitted bing cherries
1 banana, sliced

SYRUP
4 tablespoons butter
1/2 cup firmly packed brown sugar
1/2 cup applesauce
1/4 cup Amaretto

TOPPING
1 cup chopped pecans
4 tablespoons brown sugar

Preheat oven to 325° F. Drain fruit cocktail and mix with cherries and banana slices in a 9x13-inch baking pan. In a saucepan, mix butter, brown sugar, applesauce, and Amaretto. Bring to a slow boil, remove from heat, and pour over fruit. Top with pecans and brown sugar and bake for 1 hour. Serve hot.

**The canned fruit cocktail makes this quick. You may want to substitute 7 cups diced fresh fruits: peaches, apples, pears, pineapple, and grapes.*

Oak Square

Port Gibson, Mississippi

Thanks to a moment of sentimentality in the heart of Ulysses S. Grant, this majestic plantation home still stands. The year: 1863. The occasion: Grant moves his troops through Port Gibson, but decides the town is "too beautiful to burn."

It was such a setting that the original builder selected for this Greek Revival-style mansion in 1850 (it is listed on the National Register of Historic Places). Outside, the front gallery is supported by Corinthian columns twenty-two feet tall. Inside are palatial rooms, massive sliding doors, specially designed centerpieces, and ornate millwork. Throughout the house is displayed a rare collection of memorabilia from Civil War days, including family heirlooms.

Martha and William Lum—owners of Oak Square—trace their Mississippi ancestry back more than two hundred years and are themselves a rich repository of local history.

The finely appointed guest house has a four-poster canopied bed, luxurious carpeting, and furnishings that exemplify the grandeur of antebellum days.

Oak Square's Southern plantation breakfast would have given pause even to Grant: buttermilk biscuits, cheese grits, Mississippi ham, and specially prepared egg dishes.

CHEESE GRITS

Serves six to eight

1 cup quick-cooking grits
4 cups water
1 teaspoon salt
8 ounces American cheese, cubed
4 tablespoons butter or margarine, softened
2 eggs
1/2 cup milk (approximate)

Preheat oven to 350° F. Stir grits into boiling, salted water. Cover and cook 5 minutes, stirring occasionally to insure smooth consistency. Remove from heat. Add cheese and butter; mix thoroughly until melted. Crack eggs into a measuring cup and beat with a fork. Add enough milk to make 1 cup. Mix well and add gradually to the grits. Bake in a greased casserole for 30–40 minutes.

SOUTHERN BUTTERMILK BISCUITS

Makes twelve biscuits
2 cups all-purpose flour
3 teaspoons baking powder
1/2 teaspoon salt
4 tablespoons shortening
1/2 teaspoon baking soda
1 cup buttermilk

Preheat oven to 450° F. Sift and mix flour, baking powder, and salt. Cut in shortening with a pastry blender. Mix soda with buttermilk, slowly add to the flour mixture and mix to make a soft dough. Roll out on a floured board to 1/2-inch thickness and cut with a biscuit cutter. Bake on an ungreased cookie sheet 10–12 minutes.

Folkestone Lodge

Bryson City, North Carolina

A small, secluded, old-fashioned inn that offers a quiet retreat in a rural setting. Home-cooked family breakfasts. Cozy guest rooms. That's Folkestone Lodge.

Built in 1926 as a farmhouse, this rustic inn is located just a quarter mile from one of the entrances to the Great Smoky Mountain National Park. Its five guest rooms are furnished in a manner reminiscent of an earlier time and a long-forgotten lifestyle. Rooms have beds with high headboards and hand-crocheted spreads; the baths have antique washstands and claw-foot tubs.

Breakfast—featuring fresh breads, Grandma's Old-Fashioned Oatmeal, eggs and other treats—is served in a glassed-in dining room with a breathtaking view of the surrounding mountains.

BREAKFAST FELLOWSHIP
AT FOLKESTONE LODGE

Fresh Fruit in Season

Blueberry Muffins

Bacon and Eggs

Cheese Grits

Grandma's Old-Fashioned Oatmeal

GRANDMA'S OLD-FASHIONED OATMEAL

Serves six

2-1/2 cups water
1/8 teaspoon salt
2 cups quick-cooking oatmeal
2 tablespoons sugar
1/2 teaspoon ground cinnamon
One 5-ounce can condensed milk
3 tablespoons butter
5 tablespoons brown sugar

Bring water to a boil; add salt. Stirring constantly, add oats, sugar, and cinnamon. Cook 1 minute. Add condensed milk and reheat to boiling state. Pour into serving dish and top with butter and brown sugar.

The Conyers House

Sperryville, Virginia

Previously known as Conyers' old store, Finks' general store, and a hippie hangout, this historic late 1700s farmhouse was resurrected as a family country home by Sandra and Norman Cartwright-Brown in 1979. Just two years later the self-declared innkeepers opened their doors to receive their first paying guests.

The accommodations, named for important personages in the family history, are laden with antiques including a seventh-generation family rocking chair, a walnut wardrobe circa 1830, an 1820 rope bed, and a Mission oak sofa.

Being located in the foothills of the Blue Ridge Mountains, the inn attracts hikers, horse lovers, fox hunters, antiques buffs, connoisseurs of fine wine, and plain country folk. The world's biggest and (purportedly) best forty-cent ice cream cone can be had just three miles away. Swimming, tubing, and canoeing in the Hughes River are possible if they're not baptizin'.

Recipes featured here are more often than not part of the inn's "Fox and Hounds" post-hunt buffet. The red pepper jelly, slathered on bagels with cream cheese, elicits ooh's and ah's. Conyers House Parsnip Cake is a Sandra Cartwright-Brown original, and the Buckwheat Crêpes with Sausage and Apple Stuffing were especially developed for The Conyers House by Richard Mahan, chef at The Inn at Little Washington.

RED PEPPER JELLY

Makes eight eight-ounce jars

5–6 red bell peppers
1 cup cider vinegar
1/2 cup lemon juice
5-1/2 cups sugar
1 teaspoon salt
1 teaspoon chili powder
6 ounces liquid pectin

Wash and seed peppers; chop in food processor or grind in blender or meat grinder. Add enough pepper pulp to the vinegar and lemon juice to make four cups. Mix in a large kettle with sugar, salt, and chili powder. Bring to a full rolling boil, stirring constantly. Remove from heat and add liquid pectin. Return to heat and boil hard for 1 minute; turn heat down to simmer. Stir and skim off foam for 5 minutes more as mixture boils gently. Pack in hot sterilized 8-ounce jars; seal and let cool on countertop. (See directions for Preserving Techniques, page 124.) Store in refrigerator up to 1 year.

BUCKWHEAT CREPES WITH SAUSAGE AND APPLE STUFFING

Serves four

BUCKWHEAT CREPES
1/4 cup all-purpose flour
2 tablespoons buckwheat flour
1 egg
1/8 teaspoon salt
1/4 cup milk
1/4 cup plus 2 tablespoons water
1 tablespoon butter, melted

Mix flours in a medium-size bowl. Add egg and salt; stir to make a stiff batter. Whisk in milk, then water, a little at a time. Finally whisk in melted butter; let batter sit 20 minutes. (Meanwhile, prepare filling.) Heat a lightly oiled skillet, griddle, or crêpe pan. For each crêpe, pour 3 tablespoons batter in pan; lift and tilt to form crêpe. Brown lightly on one side. Remove from pan; keep warm until ready to fill and serve.

FILLING
1 pound bulk pork sausage
2 tablespoons butter
3 medium apples, peeled, cored, and diced
1/2 teaspoon ground cinnamon
1/4 cup apple cider
1/2 cup sour cream
1 tablespoon fresh sage

Crumble sausage into a skillet; fry until done. Pour off all but 1 tablespoon of fat. Scoop out the sausage with a slotted spoon and set aside. Add butter to the fat left in the pan and melt over medium heat. Add diced apples, sprinkle with cinnamon, and sauté until slightly soft. Stir in apple cider and cook until cider has been reduced by half. Return sausage to the pan. Add sour cream and sage. Mix well, heating through.

ASSEMBLY Spoon filling into warm crêpes and serve immediately.

THE CONYERS HOUSE PARSNIP CAKE

Makes one cake

2-3/4 cups whole-wheat flour
1-1/2 teaspoons baking soda
1 teaspoon baking powder
1 teaspoon salt
2 eggs
1/4 pound butter, melted
2 cups sugar
1 teaspoon ground cinnamon
1 teaspoon ground nutmeg
1 teaspoon ground cloves
1 teaspoon ground allspice
1-3/4 cups applesauce
1/2 cup water
2/3 cup chopped walnuts
1 cup raisins
1 cup diced raw parsnips

ICING

1/2 cup firmly packed
  dark brown sugar
1/2 cup powdered sugar
1/4 pound butter, melted

Preheat oven to 350° F. Combine flour, soda, baking powder and salt. Whisk together eggs, butter and sugar; add to dry ingredients. Stir in remaining ingredients until thoroughly blended. Pour batter into a lightly oiled 9-inch Bundt pan and bake 40 minutes. Turn out onto a wire rack and let cool completely. Combine icing ingredients, stir until smooth, and spread on top of cake.

NATHAN BREAD

Makes one loaf

1-1/2 cups whole-wheat flour
1 teaspoon baking soda
1 teaspoon baking powder
1 teaspoon salt
Dash ground cinnamon
1 cup unprocessed bran
1/2 cup dark molasses
1/4 cup vegetable oil
1-1/2 cups buttermilk
1 tablespoon grated orange rind
Sesame seeds

Preheat oven to 375° F. Sift together flour, soda, baking powder, salt, and cinnamon. Add bran, molasses, oil, buttermilk, and orange rind; mix well. Pour batter into a lightly oiled 9x5-inch loaf pan. Sprinkle top with sesame seeds. Bake 45–50 minutes. Turn out on a wire rack and cool.

THE MIDWEST

Haus Austrian

Omena Point, Michigan

If you're accustomed to thinking of bed and breakfast in a setting of Victorians and antiques, think again. Haus Austrian is a rough-cedar contemporary that nestles in lakeside woods (there's even a private beach). The house offers two loft guest rooms with brass beds, easy chairs, and contemporary art. A Continental breakfast of home-baked goodies and fresh fruit is served in the family dining room or out on the deck overlooking the bay. Austrian hospitality is reflected in the service and the food.

AUSTRIAN MILK BREAD

Makes one large or two small loaves

8 cups all-purpose flour
2 teaspoons salt
1 tablespoon sugar
2-1/4 cups milk
4 teaspoons active dry yeast
6 tablespoons butter
1 egg yolk, mixed with 1 tablespoon water

Stir 4 cups flour with salt and sugar into a warm bowl. Stir in 1 cup milk and dry yeast. Melt butter and heat remaining milk (1-1/4 cups) over medium heat to lukewarm. Pour over flour mixture and beat 2 minutes. Add remaining flour (4 cups) and knead to a soft dough. Place dough in a buttered bowl; cover and let rise in a warm place until double in size. Divide dough into 3 parts to make 1 large braided loaf, or 6 parts to make 2 small braided loaves. Again, let rest in a warm place until doubled in size. Brush tops with egg yolk. Bake in a preheated 350° F. oven 35–40 minutes. Cool on a wire rack.

Youngs' Island

Grand Marais, Minnesota

If you want to get away from it all, you can't get much farther away than an island in Poplar Lake that overlooks Minnesota's Boundary Waters Wilderness. Youngs' Island bears the family name of Ted and Barbara Young, who live in a fifty-year-old log cabin with a guest room for two. Its country furnishings include Victorian wicker, soft Oriental rugs, and antiques which have been collected by the owners.

All of the inn's cooking is done on a wood/gas stove fired with birch and maple. That makes for not only good food, but also a cozy kitchen for morning coffee ahead of hot biscuits and baked eggs.

Because of the inn's remote location (thirty-two miles from Grand Marais), the Youngs also serve lunch and dinner. But for a real wilderness treat, take one of Ted's dog sled trips, which features trapper's stew cooked over an open fire.

YOUNGS' ISLAND BREAKFAST

Chilled Fresh Fruit Bowl

Drop Biscuits with Wild Raspberry Jam

Ted's Baked Eggs with Canadian Bacon

Poplar Fries

Trail Coffee

DROP BISCUITS

Makes twenty to twenty-four biscuits
2 cups all-purpose flour
4 teaspoons baking powder
1/2 teaspoon salt
4 tablespoons butter
1 cup milk

Preheat oven to 450° F. In a large bowl sift together flour, baking powder, and salt. Cut cold butter into the dry ingredients with a pastry blender until mixture looks like coarse cornmeal. Add milk all at once. Stir dough until just moistened. Drop from a teaspoon onto an ungreased baking sheet. Bake 12–15 minutes, until lightly browned.

WILD RASPBERRY JAM

Makes ten eight-ounce jars
3-3/4 cups fresh raspberries
6-1/2 cups sugar
1/4 cup fresh lemon juice
3-ounces liquid pectin

Sort and carefully rinse the just-picked raspberries, crush, and place 3-3/4 cups crushed berries into a large kettle. Add sugar and lemon juice; stir well. Place over high heat and quickly bring to a boil until bubbles appear all over the surface. Boil hard for 1 minute, stirring constantly. Remove from heat. Add liquid pectin, stir, and skim off foam with a metal spoon. Immediately fill hot, sterilized 8-ounce jars, seal, and process in a water bath for 5 minutes. (See directions for Preserving Techniques, page 124.)

TED'S BAKED EGGS WITH CANADIAN BACON

Serves four
4 eggs
1 cup milk
2 tablespoons butter
1/4 cup chopped mushrooms
1/4 cup chopped green bell peppers
1/4 cup chopped onions
4 slices Canadian bacon
Ground or freshly grated nutmeg

Preheat oven to 325° F. In a large bowl, mix together eggs and milk; beat until frothy. Melt butter in a skillet over low heat. Sauté mushrooms, green peppers, and onions until limp. Stir sautéed vegetables into egg mixture and pour into a buttered 8x8-inch baking dish. Place slices of Canadian bacon on top of the egg mixture. Sprinkle with nutmeg. Bake 20 minutes, uncovered, until eggs are set.

Thorwood Bed & Breakfast

Hastings, Minnesota

After surviving a tenure as both a hospital and an apartment house, this French, Second Empire-style dwelling was purchased for use as an inn. Owners Pam and Dick Thorsen lovingly refer to their home (now listed on the National Register of Historic Places) as a "restoration in progress" that they share with family, guests, and friends.

There are no TVs or radios here, but each suite-sized room has its own wind-up Victrola. Rooms also have separate dining areas so guests can enjoy intimate breakfasts from the homemade goodies and local specialties delivered to their door in a decorative wicker basket.

Thorwood is located two blocks from the Mississippi in this river town, which is only forty minutes from the Twin Cities of Minneapolis/St. Paul.

A TISKET, A TASKET
A THORWOOD BREAKFAST BASKET

Fresh Fruit Platter

Cinnamon Toast

Ham Roll-Ups

Poppyseed Muffins

Fresh Orange Juice

Coffee or Tea

A "Good Morning" Note

Fresh Flowers

The Local Paper

HAM ROLL-UPS

Serves four

12 thin slices cooked ham
One 8-ounce package cream cheese, softened
1/4 cup mango chutney
Parsley sprigs

Spread each slice of ham with 1 tablespoon cream cheese and 1–2 teaspoons chutney. Roll into cylinders and arrange on a platter with sprigs of parsley.

POPPYSEED MUFFINS

Makes two dozen muffins

2-1/2 cups sugar
2 cups evaporated milk
5 eggs
1/2 cup milk
5 cups all-purpose flour
4-1/2 teaspoons baking powder
1/2 teaspoon salt
1/2 cup poppyseeds
1-1/2 teaspoons vanilla extract

Preheat oven to 350° F. Combine sugar, evaporated milk, eggs, and milk. In a separate bowl sift together flour, baking powder, and salt. Add wet ingredients to dry, then mix in poppyseeds and vanilla. Beat until smooth. Pour batter into greased muffin tins (3/4 full) and bake 40 minutes. Serve warm.

The Rahilly House

Lake City, Minnesota

Through the many periods of Lake City's development from frontier to agrarian to industrial to semi-resort town, the Rahilly House has stood proudly since 1868 as a fine example of Classic Greek Revival architecture. It has also had some locally eminent owners: a postmaster, a newspaper editor, a state senator, a Ziegfeld Follies entertainer. Listed in the National Historical Register, this luxurious home is today a quiet guest house. Its comfortable rooms are tastefully furnished with antiques, cozy beds, and soft comforters.

Guests can enjoy a crackling fireplace in the parlor while savoring a glass of afternoon wine. Breakfast, served in the sunny dining room, is a hearty country affair consisting of Cookie Crust Fruit Baskets, Pumpkin Date Muffins, eggs, and other homemade specialties.

FROM THE RAHILLY HOUSE KITCHEN

Cookie Crust Fruit Basket

Pumpkin Date Muffins

Creamy Eggs and Asparagus

Bacon and Sausage

Juice and Coffee

COOKIE CRUST FRUIT BASKET

Makes eight to ten baskets

1/4 pound butter
1/2 cup sugar
1/4 cup corn syrup
1/4 cup light molasses
7 tablespoons all-purpose flour
1 cup finely chopped pecans
2 teaspoons vanilla extract

Plain yogurt
Sliced fresh fruit

Preheat oven to 325° F. Melt butter in a saucepan over low heat. Add sugar, corn syrup, and molasses. Cook over high heat, stirring constantly, until liquid boils. Remove from heat and stir in flour, nuts, and vanilla. For each basket spoon 2–3 tablespoons batter onto the center of a well-greased baking sheet. Bake, one at a time, until rich golden brown; about 10–11 minutes. (Batter will thin and spread considerably.)

Remove from oven; let cool until cookie firms up slightly, about 1 minute. When edges are just firm enough to lift (but still warm and pliable), lift cookie, turn and drape it over a glass that measures approximately 2 inches across the bottom. Gently cup cookie around the base. Let shaped cookie cool until firm. (Note: Timing is crucial. If the cookie is lifted too soon, it will continue to spread and fall apart; if allowed to cool too long, it loses its flexibility and sticks to the pan. Expect to lose one or two "practicing.") Baskets can be stored in an airtight container at room temperature for up to one week.

When ready to serve, put a scoop of plain yogurt in each basket. Top with sliced fresh fruit.

PUMPKIN DATE MUFFINS

Makes fifteen muffins

3/4 cup packed brown sugar
1/4 pound butter, softened
1/4 cup light molasses
1 egg, slightly beaten
1 cup canned pumpkin
1-3/4 cups all-purpose flour
1 teaspoon baking soda
1/4 teaspoon salt
1/2 teaspoon ground cinnamon
1/4 teaspoon ground nutmeg
1/2 cup chopped dates

Preheat oven to 350° F. Cream sugar, butter, and molasses. Add egg and pumpkin; beat until smooth. Stir together remaining ingredients in a separate mixing bowl. Add to pumpkin mixture, stirring until just moistened (batter will be lumpy). Spoon into lightly greased muffin tins (1/2 full). Bake 20 minutes.

CREAMY EGGS AND ASPARAGUS

Serves four

3 tablespoons butter
3 tablespoons all-purpose flour
1-3/4 cups milk
Dash salt
Dash white pepper
1/2 cup grated sharp Cheddar cheese
5 hard-cooked eggs, sliced
4 English muffins, toasted
16 fresh asparagus spears, steamed
Paprika

Melt butter in a saucepan. Blend in flour, add milk, cook and stir until thickened. Season with salt and pepper. Add cheese; stir and blend until melted. Remove from heat. Fold in sliced eggs. Serve over toasted English muffins. Arrange steamed asparagus spears on top. Sprinkle with paprika. Serve hot.

Canterbury Inn

Rochester, Minnesota

Chaucer told of ailing pilgrims on their way to Canterbury Cathedral stopping over at the English town of Rochester. Not so coincidentally, visitors to the Mayo Clinic in Rochester, Minnesota, can stop over at the Canterbury Inn. This warm bed and breakfast house is kept by Mary Martin and Jeffrey Van Sant, two dedicated people with backgrounds in nursing and church work.

The Victorian building was constructed in 1890 as a family residence and later served as a restaurant. Mary and Jeffrey purchased it in 1982, restored its handsome woodwork, stained glass, and gingerbread trim, and turned it into Rochester's first B&B. Four guest rooms offer king, queen or twin-sized beds.

The Rochester area offers hiking, biking, and cross-country skiing, but—since Mary and Jeffrey are oriented to taking care of people—why not relax and be spoiled?

A full breakfast is presented in the dining room, or—if you really want to indulge yourself—served at bedside from six-thirty to noon. In the late afternoon you'll find tea, coffee, wine, and snacks in the parlor.

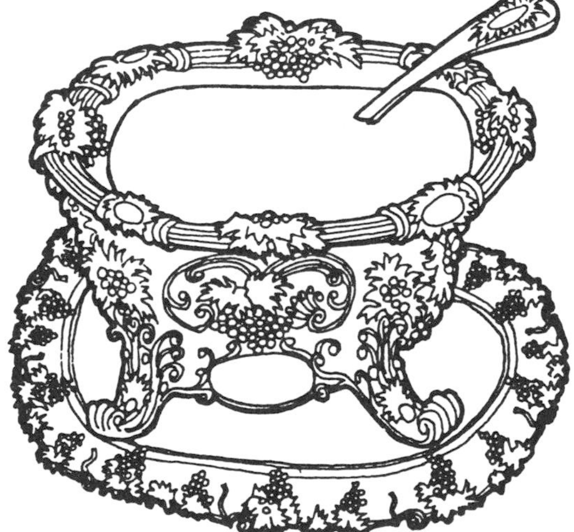

MINNESOTA WILD RICE WAFFLES

Makes ten waffles

3 eggs, separated
1-1/2 cups milk
1-3/4 cups sifted all-purpose flour
4 teaspoons baking powder
1/2 teaspoon salt
1/4 pound butter, melted
1 cup cooked wild rice
Maple syrup

Beat egg yolks with a fork or wire whisk; stir in milk, flour, baking powder, salt, and melted butter. Mix until smooth and stir in cooked wild rice. Beat egg whites until they form stiff peaks and fold into batter. Bake in a hot waffle iron. Serve with maple syrup.

GINGERBREAD WAFFLES

Makes ten waffles

3 eggs, separated
1 cup milk
1/2 cup dark molasses
1/2 cup firmly packed brown sugar
1-3/4 cups all-purpose flour
4 teaspoons baking powder
1/2 teaspoon salt
1 teaspoon ground cinnamon
1 teaspoon ground ginger
1/4 teaspoon ground cloves
1/4 pound butter, melted
Lemon Curd or Ginger Whipped Cream, following

Beat egg yolks with a fork or wire whisk; add in milk, molasses and brown sugar and mix well. In a separate mixing bowl sift together flour, baking powder, salt, and spices. Add liquid ingredients to dry, along with melted butter; mix until blended. Beat egg whites until they form stiff peaks and fold into batter. Bake in a hot waffle iron. Serve with Lemon Curd or Ginger Whipped Cream.

LEMON CURD

Makes three cups

3 eggs
6 tablespoons butter
7/8 cup sugar
Grated rind and juice of 2 lemons

Slightly beat eggs in the top of a double boiler away from heat. Add butter, sugar, lemon rind, and juice. Set over boiling water and stir constantly until mixture is slightly thickened and smooth. Pour into 3 warm 8-ounce jars. Cool. Cap and refrigerate until ready to use. Will keep several weeks.

GINGER WHIPPED CREAM

Makes one cup

2 tablespoons sugar
1 cup heavy cream
2 tablespoons finely chopped, crystallized ginger

Add sugar to cream and whip to form soft peaks. Fold in crystallized ginger. Serve with Gingerbread Waffles.

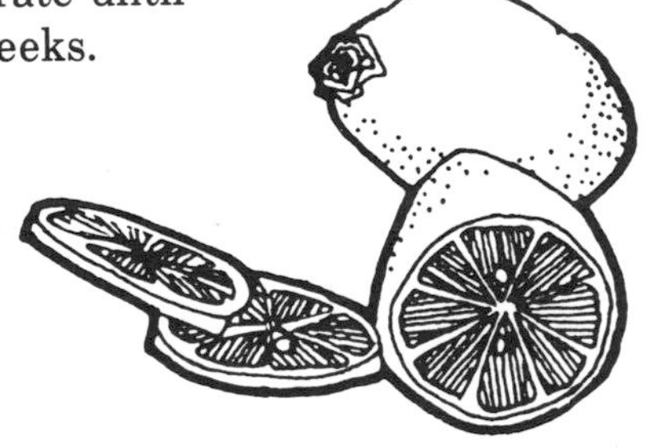

THE SOUTHWEST

1899 Inn

La Veta, Colorado

Marilyn Hall was an activity coordinator for a retirement center in Colorado Springs when *she* got the bug to "retire" to the southeastern Colorado town of La Veta at the base of the Spanish Peaks.

Here she purchased a rustic stone house and eventually transformed it into a five-guest-room bed and breakfast inn. The decor runs to Early American. Windows from the La Veta Room look out to Greenhorn Mountain; from the Trinchera Room guests view Trinchera Peak.

Marilyn describes the inn as a place where "you can take off your shoes and feel right at home." But for those of a more ambitious nature golfing, horseback riding, backpacking, skiing, and snowmobiling are the activities available.

BRAN MUFFINS

Makes eighteen muffins

1 cup boiling water
2-3/4 cups Kellogg's Bran Buds cereal
1/4 cup maple syrup
1/2 teaspoon salt
1/2 cup vegetable oil
2 eggs
1-1/2 cups buttermilk
2-1/2 teaspoons baking soda
2-1/2 cups whole-wheat pastry flour
1 cup raisins
Pecan pieces
Brown sugar

Preheat oven to 400° F. Pour boiling water over cereal and soak 15–20 minutes. Combine syrup, salt, oil, eggs, buttermilk, soda, and flour in a large mixing bowl. Mix thoroughly. Stir in raisins. Finally add cereal and mix well. Spoon batter into greased muffin tins (3/4 full). Top with pecan pieces and sprinkle with brown sugar. Bake 20 minutes.

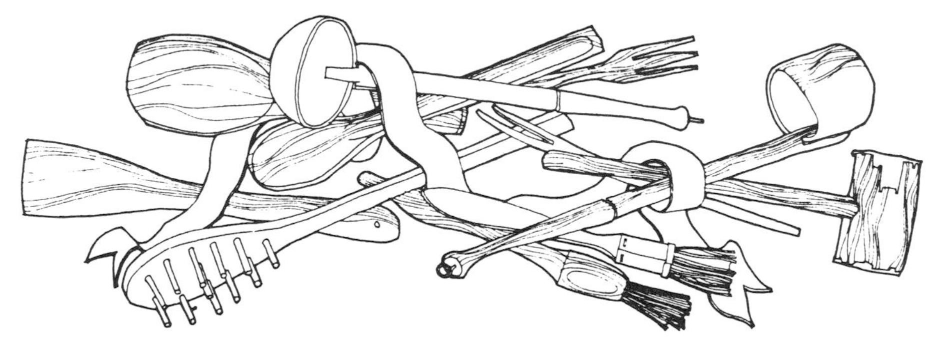

The Plum Tree

Pilar, New Mexico

The Plum Tree is what's called a budget B&B; otherwise known as a bed and breakfast hostel. For $10 a night "bring-your-own-sleeping-bag" accommodations are provided. At $27.50 (per couple) the linen is supplied.

Four adobe-style buildings comprise the inn complex. One houses the sleeping quarters, another a cafe; the third is a combination home/art studio for innkeeper Dick Thibodeau and wife Karen; the fourth is the site of the inn's sauna, hot tub, and massage facilities. Apple, apricot, peach, and plum orchards surround the property, which draws artists, writers, and musicians as its primary clientele.

Fine arts workshops are offered at The Plum Tree throughout the summer. Day-long hiking or skiing tours leave here each Monday morning. The Taos ski basin is just forty-five minutes away; Santa Fe is fifty miles to the south.

A PLUM GOOD BREAKFAST
AT THE PLUM TREE

Freshly Squeezed Orange Juice

Green Chili Scrambled Tofu

Home Fried Potatoes

Apricot-Banana Coffeecake

Steaming Hot Coffee

GREEN CHILI SCRAMBLED TOFU

Serves six

2 tablespoons vegetable oil
3/4 cup chopped onion
1/2 cup diced tomato
2 cloves garlic, minced
2 pounds tofu, crumbled
3 tablespoons soy sauce
2 tablespoons Dijon-style mustard
1 tablespoon brewer's yeast
1/4 cup diced green Ortega chili peppers

Heat oil in a large frying pan. Sauté onion, tomato, and garlic together until tender. Add tofu, soy sauce, mustard, yeast, and chilies. Mix well and continue cooking until heated through. Serve hot.

APRICOT-BANANA COFFEECAKE

Makes one large cake

3/4 cup butter
1-1/2 cups honey
3/4 cup milk
3 eggs, lightly beaten
2 cups mashed ripe bananas
1-1/2 teaspoons vanilla extract
1/2 teaspoon lemon extract
2 cups whole-wheat pastry flour
1-1/2 cups all-purpose flour
3 teaspoons baking powder
1 teaspoon baking soda
1-1/2 teaspoons ground cinnamon
1/2 teaspoon ground nutmeg

FILLING
1-1/2 cups chopped fresh apricots
3/4 cup honey
1 teaspoon vanilla extract
2 tablespoons cornstarch

Preheat oven to 350° F. Melt butter in a large saucepan, then add honey, milk, eggs, bananas, vanilla, and lemon extract; whisk together. In a large mixing bowl, stir together flours, baking powder, soda, cinnamon, and nutmeg. Add wet ingredients to dry; mix well. Pour batter into a greased 9x13-inch baking dish. Set aside.

To prepare filling, combine apricots, honey, and vanilla in a saucepan. Bring to a slow boil, then reduce heat and simmer, stirring frequently, until clear. Mix cornstarch with just enough water to dissolve. Add to apricot mixture and stir over low heat until thickened. Remove from heat and allow to cool. Spoon into cake batter to form 3 rows running the length of the pan. Bake 45 minutes.

Grant Corner Inn

Santa Fe, New Mexico

Located just two blocks from Santa Fe's historic downtown plaza, Grant Corner Inn offers bed and breakfast in a Colonial manor built at the turn of the century for the wealthy Windsor family. The inn's nine guest rooms are appointed with antiques and treasures from around the world. Armoires, handmade quilts, brass beds, and four-posters are much in evidence.

In accordance with the European tradition of bed and breakfast, the morning meal is served before a crackling fire in the dining room or on the veranda during the summer months. The varied menu (posted on the dining room mantle the night before) includes such delights as New Mexican soufflé, banana waffles, or Zucchini Egg Ramekins smothered with cheese sauce (as presented here). This hearty main dish is accompanied with home-baked rolls or muffins (cherry prove to be a favorite), freshly squeezed juice or a blended fruit drink (such as Apricot-Banana Frappé) and freshly ground European coffee.

BREAKFAST AT GRANT CORNER INN

Apricot-Banana Frappé

Cantaloupe Wedges topped with Kiwi

Zucchini Egg Ramekins with Cheese Sauce

Fresh Cherry Muffins

Coffee or Tea

APRICOT-BANANA FRAPPE

*Makes six cups**

3 cups apricot nectar
1/2 cup fresh orange juice
2 tablespoons lemon juice
1/4 cup cream
1/4 cup plain yogurt
2 ripe bananas, sliced
1 cup crushed ice
Fresh mint sprigs

Mix all ingredients except mint in blender for 1 minute on high speed. Serve in frosted goblets garnished with fresh mint sprigs.

**Be sure your blender holds 6 cups or more; if smaller, make recipe in 2 batches.*

ZUCCHINI EGG RAMEKINS WITH CHEESE SAUCE

Serves six

1 small yellow onion, chopped
2 cloves garlic, minced
4 tablespoons butter
4 small zucchini, sliced
10 mushrooms, sliced
2 medium tomatoes, chopped
2 tablespoons chopped fresh parsley
1 tablespoon chopped fresh cilantro
1 teaspoon salt
6 slices bacon, cooked and crumbled
12 eggs, poached
Cheese Sauce, following page

Sauté onion and garlic in butter until golden then add zucchini, mushrooms, and tomatoes. Cook until tender. Add herbs, salt, and bacon. Drain liquid from the mixture and divide into 6 individual ramekins. Place 2 poached eggs in each ramekin and top with cheese sauce.

CHEESE SAUCE

2 tablespoons butter
3 tablespoons all-purpose flour
2 cups milk
2 cups grated Monterey Jack cheese
1/2 teaspoon salt
1/4 teaspoon dry mustard
1/4 teaspoon cayenne

Melt butter in heavy saucepan over medium heat. Stir in flour and cook while stirring for several minutes. Add milk, stirring constantly until sauce is thick and bubbly. Stir in cheese and seasonings and cook until cheese is melted.

FRESH CHERRY MUFFINS

Makes twenty-four muffins
1/4 pound unsalted butter, softened
2 eggs
1-1/2 cups sugar
3 cups all-purpose flour
2-1/2 teaspoons baking powder
1/2 teaspoon salt
Pinch baking soda
1 teaspoon vanilla extract
1 cup milk
2 cups fresh cherries, pitted

Preheat oven to 400° F. Cream butter, eggs, and sugar together in a large bowl. In a medium-size bowl combine flour, baking powder, salt, and baking soda. Add vanilla to milk. Alternately add milk then flour mixture to creamed butter mixture and mix well. Fold cherries into batter. Spoon into oiled muffin tins (1/2–3/4 full) and bake for 15–20 minutes, or until golden brown.

Rancho Arriba

Truchas, New Mexico

Situated on the "High Road To Taos" and El Camino Real is Truchas, an adobe village settled in 1752. At eight thousand feet above sea level, Truchas lies in the Royal Land Grant—Nuestra Señora Del Rosario San Fernando y Santiago. Gateway to the Carson National Forest and Pecos Wilderness, the area offers numerous recreational opportunities and diverse accommodations as well.

Among these is Rancho Arriba, a small working farm that is also a B&B, run by innkeepers Curtiss and Jessica Frank. Their guest house is equipped with three bedrooms and a large airy dining room/parlor with a corner fireplace. But the hub of activity is the kitchen, where croissants and Danish pastries are baked each morning, new-laid eggs are prepared on a wood cookstove, and a special blend of house coffee with ground garbanzo beans is served with real cream.

GREEN EGGS AND HAM

Serves four

1-1/2 cups thinly julienned or
  finely shredded ham
1 avocado, peeled and pitted
1 pint sour cream
8 eggs, poached
4 English muffins, halved and toasted

Preheat oven to 250° F. and warm ham. In a blender purée avocado with sour cream. Place a poached egg on each toasted English muffin half. Cover with avocado sauce and top with warm ham.

BUTTERFLIES

Makes fifteen pastries

3/4 pound cold unsalted butter
3-1/4 cups all-purpose flour
Two 1/4-ounce packages active dry yeast
1/4 cup lukewarm water
2 eggs, lightly beaten
1/2 cup evaporated milk
1/4 cup sugar
1 teaspoon salt

POPPY SEED FILLING*
6 tablespoons butter, softened
6 tablespoons honey
2/3 cup poppy seeds
1 cup ground walnuts or pecans
2 tablespoons freshly grated orange peel
2–3 tablespoons heavy cream

PASTRY Cut small chunks of the butter into 2 cups of flour with a pastry blender, or process in a food processor until particles are the size of peas. Stir in remaining flour (1-1/4 cups). Set aside. Dissolve yeast in warm water; stir in eggs, milk, sugar, and salt. Let stand until bubbly, approximately 12–15 minutes. Pour liquids into flour; stir until just moistened. Cover and refrigerate overnight.

FILLING Cream together butter and honey. Blend in poppy seeds, nuts, citrus peel, and enough heavy cream to make spreading consistency. (May be refrigerated in a covered jar for up to several days. Bring to room temperature before using.)

ASSEMBLY Preheat oven to 400° F. Roll pastry out to an 8x16-inch rectangle. Spread poppy seed filling over pastry and roll "jelly-roll" fashion, beginning with the long side. Cut crosswise into 1-inch slices. Fit 2 slices, cut side up, side-by-side into an English muffin ring** placed on an ungreased cookie sheet. The slices should fit together to resemble butterfly wings, touching in the center. Let rest 10 minutes. Bake 15 minutes, until lightly golden brown. Cool slightly on a wire rack and spread with Almond Buttercream Icing.

**A commercial poppy seed filling such as a 12-1/2-ounce can of Solo brand may be substituted.*

***English muffin rings are available in gourmet cookware stores.*

ALMOND BUTTERCREAM ICING

1/4 pound cold butter
1 cup powdered sugar
1 teaspoon almond extract
6 tablespoons heavy cream

Cut butter into chunks. Mix with remaining ingredients in food processor or with a mixer until smooth. Spread on slightly warm Butterflies.

Traveler's Hotel

Denison, Texas

Just two years ago Bob and Betty Brandt purchased this historic hotel, constructed by a German sea captain in 1893. Today its turn-of-the-century antique-filled guest rooms and award-winning restaurant host out-of-state travelers, as well as local politicians and celebrities. The Brandt's serve their guests breakfast in bed, a tradition that reflects not only the inn's European heritage, but their own special brand of Texas hospitality. Crackers and Eggs is a recipe that has been handed down through Betty's family.

CRACKERS AND EGGS

Serves four

2 eggs
1 cup milk
One 4-ounce package saltine crackers
4 tablespoons butter
Maple syrup

Beat eggs and milk together with a fork or wire whisk until completely blended. Crumble crackers into bowl containing egg/milk mixture and stir gently. (Batter will be lumpy.) Melt butter in skillet over medium heat, being careful not to burn it. Pour egg and cracker mixture into skillet. Cook covered for approximately 5 minutes. Flip over and cook for another 5–7 minutes, until done. Cut into 4 wedges. Serve immediately with warm butter and maple syrup.

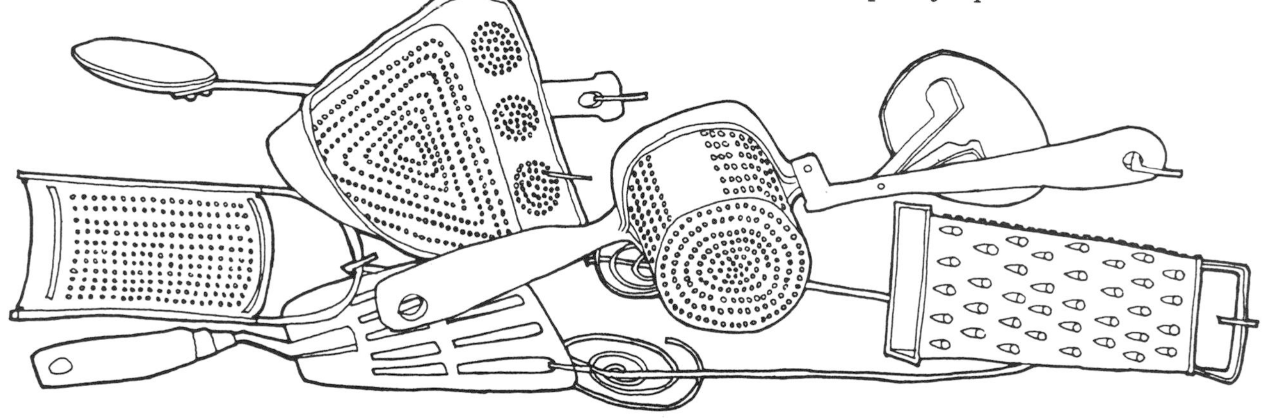

The Old Miners' Lodge

Park City, Utah

This narrow, two-story structure was built in 1893 as a boardinghouse to accommodate men working the local silver mines. Seventy-five years later it housed twentieth-century apartment dwellers. Today it is a bed and breakfast inn whose owners are dedicated to providing "creature comforts" for their guests.

The Old Miners' Lodge is located in the historical section of Park City overlooking the magnificent Wasatch Valley. Its spirit is casual and private. Seven guest rooms—named after local historical characters—are well appointed and comfortable. There is a big brass bed, a wood-paneled bath, rocking chairs, and view windows. Mining artifacts are mixed with Victorian pieces, and in the old-fashioned parlor are books, games, and a cozy fireplace.

Breakfast—with a hearty and varied menu—is served in the parlor from eight to nine. The favorite spread features the lodge's own version of Mexican-style eggs, potatoes, and fresh raspberries; others include German pancakes, banana waffles, eggs Benedict with crab, crêpes, and blintzes.

MEXICAN EGG BURRITOS

Serves six

SALSA
3 large tomatoes, chopped
2–3 tablespoons chopped Ortega chilies
1/2 cup chopped white onion
1 clove garlic, pressed
4–5 tablespoons chopped fresh cilantro

6 flour tortillas
2 tablespoons butter
10 eggs
1/2 cup light cream
4 ounces sharp Cheddar cheese, grated
1/2 pint sour cream
Pepper
One 4-ounce can chopped ripe olives
3 green onions, sliced
1 large tomato, thinly sliced
1 ripe avocado, sliced

Combine salsa ingredients and set aside. Steam tortillas on a wire rack over boiling water for 1 minute on each side. Meanwhile, melt butter in a large skillet. Beat eggs with cream, pour into skillet and scramble gently. Stir in cheese and cook until melted. Lay scrambled eggs on top of hot tortillas. Spoon on salsa, a dollop of sour cream, dash of pepper, some olives and onions. Garnish with tomato and avocado slices.

CALIFORNIA

Rose Victorian Inn

The Carter House

The Grey Whale Inn

Campbell Ranch Inn

Hope-Merrill House

San Benito House

Grape Leaf Inn

The Heirloom

The Beazley House

La Maida House

The Fleming Jones Homestead

The Glenborough Inn

The Cinnamon Bear

The Foxes

Rose Victorian Inn

Arroyo Grande, California

The Rose Victorian Inn, painted four shades of rose, is a haven for writers, movie producers, celebrities, and top government officials (their autographed pictures line the wall of the inn's adjoining restaurant and bar). Oak, mahogany, and rosewood antiques fill the fourteen rooms of this Eastlake Stick-style Victorian, which formerly served as the homestead of a large walnut farm.

While this full-service country inn on California's central coast is hard to leave, you won't have to—at least not for a while. The accommodations include breakfast *and* dinner. Iced tea and hors d'oeuvre are set out in the early afternoon. There's a pump organ in the parlor, croquet on the lawn, a grand piano in the living room, and an antiques shop on the grounds.

ROMANTIC RENDEZVOUS AT THE ROSE VICTORIAN

Eggs Benedict

Fresh Fruit Plate
Melons, Oranges, Kiwi, Berries

Pecan Sour Cream Coffeecake

Whipped Butter and Homemade Jams

A Mimosa
(Half Orange Juice, Half Champagne)

Freshly Roasted Coffee

EGGS BENEDICT

Serves four
2 English muffins, halved, toasted, and buttered
4 slices Canadian bacon, cooked
4 eggs, poached
Hollandaise, following

Top each muffin half with a slice of bacon and a poached egg. Spoon on hollandaise.

E-Z BLENDER HOLLANDAISE

Serves four to six
1/4 pound butter
3 egg yolks
1 tablespoon lemon juice
1 tablespoon dry sherry
3 dashes cayenne pepper

Melt butter to a low boiling point. Place all other ingredients in blender and blend at low speed until mixed. Slowly pour in melted butter and blend for 10 seconds, until thick and creamy. If sauce separates or is too thick, blend in water a tablespoon at a time, until it is the right consistency.

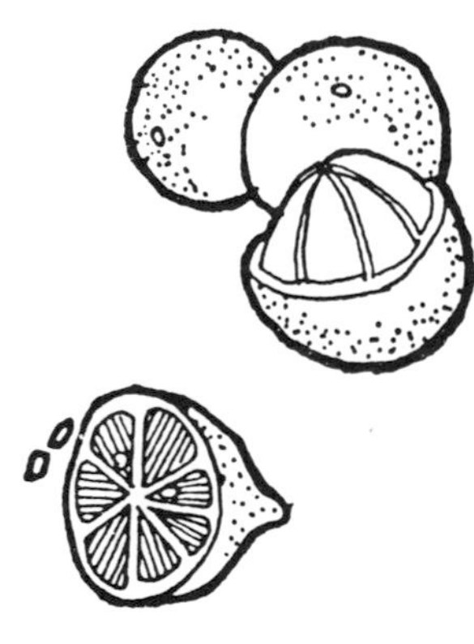

PECAN SOUR CREAM COFFEECAKE

Makes one cake

1/2 pound butter, softened
1-1/4 cups sugar
2 eggs
1/2 pint sour cream
1 teaspoon vanilla extract
2 cups all-purpose flour
1 teaspoon baking powder
1/2 teaspoon baking soda
1 cup chopped pecans
4 tablespoons sugar
1 teaspoon ground cinnamon

Preheat oven to 350° F. Beat together butter, sugar, eggs, sour cream, and vanilla; set aside. Sift together flour, baking powder and soda; add to butter/sugar mixture and mix well. Spoon half the batter into a greased and floured angelfood cake pan, distributing evenly. Sprinkle with 1/2 cup pecans, 2 tablespoons sugar, and 1/2 teaspoon cinnamon. Add remaining batter, again distributing evenly, and sprinkle with remaining pecans, sugar, and cinnamon. Bake 45 minutes. Cool 10 minutes, loosen edges, and lift out of pan.

CHEESE STRATA

Serves ten

12 slices of bread, cubed
2-1/4 cups grated sharp Cheddar cheese
12 eggs
3 cups milk
6 tablespoons butter, melted
3/4 teaspoon dry mustard

Butter a 9x13-inch baking dish. Layer bread and cheese, ending with cheese. In a mixing bowl, combine eggs, milk, melted butter and mustard; beat with a wire whisk until thoroughly mixed. Pour over bread/cheese mixture and refrigerate overnight. Preheat oven to 350° F. Bake 50–60 minutes, until firm in the center.

The Carter House

Eureka, California

A lot of charming houses built in San Francisco before the turn of the century were destroyed by the earthquake and fire of 1906. Among them was a three-story Victorian designed by the famous architects Samuel and Joseph Cather Newsom. Mark Carter happened on the original Newsom blueprints and reconstructed the home in Eureka on California's north coast. Custom-built aspects of the house include exteriors of clear heart redwood and interiors of polished redwood and oak. The main floor houses the guest lobby, antiques shop, and art gallery; the second and third floors are devoted to seven guest rooms, each furnished with period antiques.

ALMOND FILO TART

Makes one large tart

FILLING
1/2 cup unsalted butter, softened
1/2 cup sugar
1 egg
2 tablespoons dark rum
2 teaspoons almond extract
2 tablespoons all-purpose flour
2-1/2 cups finely ground blanched almonds

8 sheets filo dough
1/4 pound unsalted butter, melted
1/2 cup finely ground almonds
Powdered sugar

FILLING Cream butter and sugar with an electric mixer. Add egg, rum, almond extract and flour; beat until smooth. Fold in blanched almonds.

ASSEMBLY Preheat oven to 350° F. Lay a filo sheet across a 9-inch tart pan with removable bottom. Brush with melted butter and sprinkle with almonds. Repeat this procedure with the remaining sheets, stacking one on top of the other. Spread the filling in the last sheet to fit within dimensions of the pan. Gently fold the edges of each sheet back toward the center of the pan, brushing each with melted butter as you go. Bake for 30–35 minutes. Cool. Dust with powdered sugar.

HOMEMADE APPLESAUCE WITH WHIPPED CREAM

Makes six cups
12 tart apples, peeled, cored and chopped
1/2 cup water
1/4 cup sugar
Grated rind of 1 lemon
1/2 cup whipping cream

Place apples, water, and sugar in saucepan. Cover and cook over medium heat until apples are soft, approximately 15–20 minutes. Purée apples with lemon rind in food processor, electric mixer, or with a potato masher. Whip cream. Place 3–4 tablespoons whipped cream in a long-stemmed glass. Add 3–4 tablespoons applesauce. Garnish with a tiny flower and leaf.

The Grey Whale Inn

Fort Bragg, California

Formerly known as the Redwood Coast Hospital, the Grey Whale is now taking care of folks in a different manner. Spacious, comfortable rooms with private baths and affordable prices are central to this inn's attraction. This is not to mention a discriminating staff, a location near the area's many parks, beaches, and redwood forests—and innkeeper Colette Bailey's delicious buffet breakfast. Colette is a winner, as are her original recipes that consistently take blue ribbons at the Mendocino County Fair.

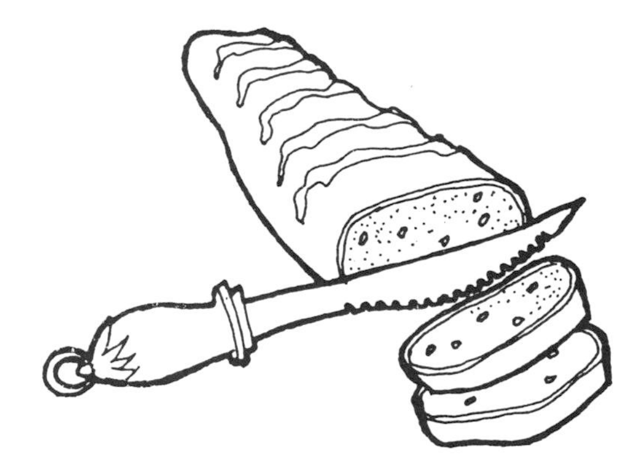

LEMON YOGURT BREAD

Makes two loaves

3 cups all-purpose flour
1 teaspoon salt
1 teaspoon baking soda
1/2 teaspoon baking powder
1 cup finely chopped blanched almonds
3 eggs
1 cup vegetable oil
1-3/4 cups sugar
1 pint lemon yogurt
1 tablespoon lemon extract

Preheat oven to 325° F. Sift together flour, salt, baking soda and baking powder. Stir in nuts and set aside. Beat eggs in a large mixing bowl. Add oil and sugar; cream well. Add lemon yogurt and extract. Combine wet and dry ingredients; beat thoroughly. Spoon batter into two well-greased 9x5-inch loaf pans or one large Bundt pan. Bake 1 hour, or until toothpick inserted in center of bread comes out clean. Cool in pan 10 minutes. Turn out onto a wire rack and continue cooling.

CHEDDAR EGGS

Serves six
8 eggs
12 ounces sharp Cheddar cheese, grated
2 teaspoons dill weed
1/2 teaspoon white pepper
1/4 teaspoon salt
2 sourdough baguettes, in 1/2-inch slices
Paprika
Parsley sprigs

Preheat oven to 375° F. Place eggs in a saucepan with warm water to cover. Bring to a boil; turn heat down and simmer 12 minutes. Drain eggs and immediately plunge into ice cold water; cover with ice. When cool, remove shells and dice eggs finely. Mix with grated cheese, dill weed, white pepper, and salt. Use a pastry blender to bring mixture to a homogeneous consistency, or blend half the mixture at a time in a food processor for 5 seconds. Mound and press approximately 2 tablespoons of mixture onto bread round, covering to the edge. Sprinkle with paprika. Place finished Cheddar-egg rounds on an ungreased baking sheet. Bake 5 minutes to melt the cheese. Serve warm, garnished with a sprig of parsley.

Campbell Ranch Inn

Geyserville, California

Bed and breakfast innkeepers Mary Jane and Jerry Campbell profess to live by the words recorded in Proverbs 11:25: A generous man will prosper; he who refreshes others will himself be refreshed.

But the "proof of the pudding" is really expressed in the day-to-day operation of their modern, split-level Campbell Ranch Inn, a place where little things mean a lot. There's homemade banana cream pie 'round the kitchen table just before bedtime, an atmosphere where family members cooperate rather than compete, and ample provisions for wholesome entertainment and recreation—a ping-pong table, tennis courts, a swimming pool, a piano, bicycles, and billiards.

This is California wine country in all its splendor; picturesque views of lush rolling vineyards and winery tours abound.

RANCH HAND'S REQUEST AT THE CAMPBELL RANCH

Casaba Melon
with Fresh Strawberries and Mint

The Campbell Ranch Egg Puff

Homemade Honey Wheat Loaf
with Butter and Jam

Coffee, Tea, and Hot Chocolate

THE CAMPBELL RANCH EGG PUFF

Serves eight to ten

1/4 pound butter
1 pound fresh mushrooms, chopped
10 large eggs
1 pint cottage cheese
1 pound Monterey Jack cheese, grated
1/2 cup all-purpose flour
1 teaspoon baking powder
1/2 teaspoon salt

Preheat oven to 350° F. Melt butter in a large frying pan. Remove from heat and cool slightly. Add mushrooms and toss gently to coat (do not sauté); set aside. Beat eggs in a large mixing bowl. Add cottage cheese, Monterey Jack, flour, baking powder, and salt. Mix thoroughly. Stir in mushrooms. Pour into a greased 9x13-inch baking dish, or 9 individual ramekins able to hold 3/4 cup each. Bake 45–50 minutes.

HOMEMADE HONEY WHEAT LOAVES

Makes six small loaves

1-1/2 cups boiling water
1 cup rolled oats
3/4 cup honey
3 tablespoons butter, softened
2 teaspoons salt
One 1/4-ounce package active dry yeast
2 cups lukewarm water
1 cup seven-grain cereal
3 cups whole-wheat flour
4 cups all-purpose flour
Melted butter

Pour boiling water over the oats; let stand 30 minutes. Add honey, butter, and salt; set aside. Dissolve yeast in warm water and add to the oat mixture. Beat and work in the seven-grain cereal and whole-wheat flour. Then add the all-purpose flour to make a medium-soft dough. Turn onto a floured board and knead for 10 minutes (adding flour to keep the dough from sticking). The dough should be smooth and elastic. Place dough in an oiled bowl; oil top of dough. Cover with a towel and let rise until double in bulk, at least 1 hour. Turn onto floured board and knead again. Divide the dough into 6 equal portions. Shape into small loaves and place into 6 oiled 5x3x2-inch foil loaf pans. Fit the pans onto a large cookie sheet, cover with a towel, and let rise until double in size (approximately 30 minutes).

Preheat oven to 400° F. Bake loaves 5 minutes. Lower heat to 350° F. and bake 25–30 minutes longer, until loaves sound hollow when tapped. Immediately remove from pans onto wire cooling racks and brush tops with butter. Serve warm or wrap in foil when completely cooled and freeze.

Hope-Merrill House

Geyserville, California

Geyserville's Hope-Merrill House is a virtual museum of the Victorian era, thanks to the efforts of Bob and Rosalie Hope. They purchased the property in 1980 and set about to renovate and replicate its time down to the smallest detail. From window swags to wall coverings, perfume bottles to period porcelain, this 1875-ish Eastlake Stick-style structure offers bed and breakfast at its finest.

Guests of the inn converge in the formal dining room for a full country breakfast featuring egg dishes, homemade breads, jams and jellies, and fresh fruit. Rosalie, a caterer whose culinary talents are acclaimed throughout California's wine country, can even create a superb dish with canned cream of mushroom soup!

CHRISTMAS BREAKFAST CASSEROLE

Serves six
1 pound link sausages
4–5 slices sourdough bread, cubed
2 cups grated mild Cheddar or Monterey Jack cheese
5 eggs
3/4 teaspoon dry mustard
2-1/4 cups milk
One 10-3/4-ounce can cream of mushroom soup
1/2 soup can milk

Brown, drain, and cut up sausages. Grease a 9x13-inch baking dish. Scatter bread cubes in bottom of dish. Top with cheese and sausage; set aside. Whisk together eggs, dry mustard, and milk in a small mixing bowl. Pour over bread/cheese/sausage mixture. Cover and refrigerate overnight.

Preheat oven to 300 ° F. Dilute mushroom soup with half a soup can full of milk. Pour over casserole. Bake 1 hour, uncovered. Serve hot from the oven.

San Benito House

Half Moon Bay, California

Just forty-five minutes down the coast from San Francisco is Half Moon Bay and San Benito House, a romantic bed and breakfast inn. Originally built as a small hotel in the early 1900s, this two-story, pale blue establishment has been through a succession of owners. Today, however, it's in the capable hands of innkeeper Carol Mickelsen, whose personal touch is evident everywhere. In the twelve guest rooms are brass beds with fluffy comforters, antique dressers, and bouquets of freshly picked flowers. In addition to providing breakfast (served in your room, if you like), Carol also serves dinners nightly. The country cuisine based on coastal seafood is enhanced by vegetables and herbs from the inn's own gardens.

SAN BENITO HOUSE
EASTER BRUNCH

Champagne

Strawberry Cream Cheese Crêpes

San Benito Eggs

Fresh Asparagus

Warm Homemade Whole-Wheat Bread with Sweet Butter

Fresh Roasted Coffee

STRAWBERRY CREAM CHEESE CREPES

Makes sixteen crêpes

CREPE BATTER
1-3/4 cups all-purpose flour
1 cup cold water
1 cup milk
4 eggs
1/2 teaspoon salt
1/4 pound butter, melted

Mix together flour, water, milk, eggs, and salt. Stir in melted butter and refrigerate 1 hour. Heat a lightly oiled skillet, griddle, or crêpe pan. Spoon 3–4 tablespoons batter into pan; lift and tilt to form crêpe. Brown lightly on one side. Cool and stack between layers of waxed paper. Set aside.

CREAM CHEESE FILLING
Two 8-ounce packages cream cheese, softened
1/3 cup sugar
Juice and grated rind of 1 lemon

Beat together cream cheese, sugar, and lemon juice until fluffy. Stir in grated lemon rind.

TOPPING
6–8 cups sliced strawberries
1-1/2 cups slivered almonds

ASSEMBLY Spread completely cooled crêpes with cream cheese filling. Roll and place seam-side-down in a lightly buttered baking dish. Refrigerate until ready to serve. Preheat oven to 375° F. Place filled crêpes in oven for 10 minutes, or until softened and warm. Top with sliced strawberries and almonds. Serve immediately.

SAN BENITO EGGS

Serves eight

16 eggs, poached
16 slices Canadian bacon, fried
8 slices whole-wheat bread, toasted
2-1/2 cups Hollandaise Sauce, following
2 cups artichoke hearts, sautéed in butter

Place two slices of fried Canadian bacon on one piece toasted bread. Top with two poached eggs and Hollandaise Sauce. Garnish with sautéed artichoke hearts.

CAROL'S HOLLANDAISE SAUCE

4 egg yolks
1 tablespoon lemon juice
1/2 pound butter, cut in small chunks
1 tablespoon Dijon-style mustard
1/3 cup sour cream
Dash salt
Dash white pepper

In the top of a double boiler, whisk together egg yolks and lemon juice; gradually add the butter. Continue stirring. When mixture has thickened, add the mustard, sour cream, salt, and white pepper.

Grape Leaf Inn

Healdsburg, California

This cute Queen Anne, located in the small town of Healdsburg, is a seven-guest-room gem that has the competition worried. In keeping with its wine country setting, innkeeper Terry Sweet has named the rooms after grape varietals (Cabernet Sauvignon, Pinot Noir, Merlot, the Chardonnay suite) and decorated them along this theme. Skylights, antique armoires and whirlpool tub/showers are features the rooms have in common. A taste for Sonoma County wines and cheeses are a peculiarity guests seem to share.

The inn's full country breakfast is served around the dining room table. House specialties like Mexican eggs with guacamole and Bacon Broccoli Frittata are accompanied with fresh fruit, cereal and milk, and coffeecake or muffins.

APPLE PECAN MUFFINS

Makes one dozen muffins

2 cups whole-wheat flour
1/4 cup sugar*
1 tablespoon baking powder
1 cup milk
1/4 cup vegetable oil
1 egg
1-1/2 cups peeled and diced Red Delicious apples
1 cup chopped pecans

TOPPING
1/4 cup sugar*, mixed with
1 tablespoon ground cinnamon

Preheat oven to 400° F. Combine flour, sugar, and baking powder in a large bowl. Mix together milk, oil, and egg; stir in diced apples and pecans. Add to flour mixture and stir until just moistened. (The batter will be lumpy.) Spoon into greased muffin tins (3/4 full). Top with sugar/cinnamon mix. Bake 20–25 minutes. Serve with sweet butter and jam.

**The innkeeper uses raw (unprocessed) sugar.*

BACON BROCCOLI FRITTATA

Serves four

6 eggs
1/2 cup light cream or half-and-half
1/4 cup dry vermouth
2 cloves garlic, minced
1 small yellow onion, chopped
Dash salt
Dash pepper
1 teaspoon paprika
1/2 pound bacon, cooked and crumbled
1 head fresh broccoli flowerettes, steamed until tender
8 ounces Swiss or Gruỳre cheese, grated

Preheat oven to 350° F. Whisk together eggs, cream, and vermouth. Add garlic, onion, salt, pepper, and paprika; stir to blend. Arrange bacon and broccoli in the bottom of a buttered 8x8-inch baking dish; pour in egg mixture. Bake 20 minutes. Remove from oven, sprinkle with cheese, and continue to bake another 10 minutes, until egg mixture is set. Let cool 5 minutes in pan. Cut into squares and serve immediately.

The Heirloom

Ione, California

Built by a Southerner in 1863, this two-story brick Colonial with antebellum arch, stately columns, and white wood balconies is a prime representative of the amalgamation of architectural styles that cropped up in the Mother Lode following the Gold Rush of 1849.

Catherine and James Browning (of the famous Browning Rifle Company) lived here. So did Dr. Luther Brusi, veteran of the Confederacy. But it wasn't until 1980 that Pat Cross and Melisande Hubbs stumbled across the place after searching other areas for an appropriate dwelling to house a bed and breakfast inn.

High ceilings, paneled windows, and stained pine floors set the stage for the inn's precious antiques. One of the pieces most highly prized is a rosewood grand piano that once belonged to Lola Montez, famed "Gold Rush Queen" of the Sierra Nevada.

THE HEIRLOOM'S ROMANTIC ENGLISH GARDEN BREAKFAST

Fresh Squeezed Orange Juice

Bananas à la Patricia

Aunt Marie's Cheese Soufflé

Grandmother Katarina's Cardamom Bread

Louisiana Dark Roast Coffee

AUNT MARIE'S CHEESE SOUFFLE

Serves four

3 tablespoons butter
4 tablespoons all-purpose flour
1/4 teaspoon salt
1 cup milk
1 cup grated sharp Cheddar cheese
1/8 teaspoon cayenne
3/4 teaspoon dry mustard
1-1/2 teaspoons sugar
2 teaspoons water
3 eggs, separated

Preheat oven to 350° F. In a heavy saucepan, melt butter over low heat. Stir in flour and salt and cook a minute or so. Slowly add milk, stirring constantly. Cook and stir until thick and bubbly. Add cheese and stir until melted. Mix cayenne, dry mustard, and sugar with 2 teaspoons water to dissolve; then add to cheese sauce. Remove from heat. Stir in 3 unbeaten egg yolks. Stiffly beat egg whites and fold into sauce. Pour into an ungreased 1-quart soufflé dish or casserole. Set dish in a 1-1/2-inch bath of lukewarm water. Bake 40 minutes. Serve immediately.

GRANDMOTHER KATARINA'S CARDAMOM BREAD

Makes two loaves

1-1/4 cups milk, scalded
1/2 cup sugar
1-1/4 teaspoons salt
1 teaspoon ground cardamom
Two 1/4-ounce packages active dry yeast
1/2 cup warm water
2 eggs, slightly beaten
5-1/2 cups all-purpose flour (approximate)
1 cup chopped candied fruit
3/4 cup raisins (optional)

Pour scalded milk into a large bowl containing sugar, salt, and cardamom. Cool to lukewarm. Dissolve yeast in warm water; stir into milk mixture. Add eggs and 2 cups flour and stir to make a smooth batter. Let stand 20 minutes. Mix together candied fruit, raisins, and 2 tablespoons flour; blend into batter. Stir in enough of the remaining flour to make a soft dough. Turn onto a floured board and knead until smooth, about 5 minutes. Place in an oiled bowl, cover, and let rise in a warm place until double in size, about 1-1/2 hours. Punch down, divide into 2 large loaf portions, and let rise again until double (approximately 40–45 minutes). Bake in a preheated 350° F. oven 35–40 minutes. Turn out onto a wire rack to cool.

The Beazley House

Napa, California

The Beazleys quickly transcend the line that distinguishes innkeepers from friends. And there's no more pleasant pastime than passing time with them in their Colonial-Revival Napa residence. Built in 1902, the Beazley House contains six bedrooms, a music room, kitchen, and formal dining room. Its living room, stocked with books and games, boasts a cozy fireplace. The main house accommodates six quite nicely; two of the five rooms in the Carriage House provide two-person spas.

A tour of bed and breakfast inns of the British Isles left this California couple with a confirmed belief in the owner-occupant-operator school of innkeeping. And while Jim might indulge in an extra wink or two, Carol rises early to bake the Beazley House muffins that accompany each morning's breakfast of yogurt, cheeses, fresh fruits, hot beverages, and juice.

BEAZLEY BLUEBERRY MUFFINS

Makes sixteen muffins

2 cups all-purpose flour
1/3 cup sugar
2-1/2 teaspoons baking powder
1/2 teaspoon baking soda
1 cup fresh or frozen blueberries
1 cup buttermilk
1/3 cup vegetable oil
1 egg
Sugar

Preheat oven to 400° F. In a large bowl, mix together flour, sugar, baking powder, soda, and blueberries. In a separate container, mix buttermilk, oil, and egg. Pour wet ingredients into dry and mix quickly with a fork, until flour disappears. Do not overmix; batter should be lumpy. Spoon batter into greased muffin tins (3/4 full). Sprinkle each muffin with 1/2 teaspoon sugar. Bake 25 minutes, until just golden brown. Serve warm.

PUMPKIN BUTTERMILK MUFFINS

Makes sixteen to eighteen muffins

1/2 cup vegetable oil
1 cup sugar
2 eggs
1 cup canned pumpkin
1/3 to 1/2 cup buttermilk
2 cups all-purpose flour
2 teaspoons baking powder
1 teaspoon baking soda
1-1/2 teaspoons ground cinnamon
1/2 teaspoon ground allspice
3/4 cup chopped walnuts
1 cup raisins

Preheat oven to 350° F. Mix together oil, sugar, eggs, pumpkin, and buttermilk. Add flour, baking powder, soda, cinnamon, and allspice and beat until batter is smooth. Stir in walnuts and raisins. Spoon into greased muffin tins (3/4 full) and bake 30 minutes.

CINNAMON CRUNCH MUFFINS

Makes sixteen muffins

2 cups all-purpose flour
1/3 cup sugar
2-1/2 teaspoons baking powder
1/2 teaspoon baking soda
1 cup chopped almonds
1 cup buttermilk
1/3 cup vegetable oil
1 egg
1 tablespoon ground cinnamon mixed with 1/4 cup sugar

Preheat oven to 400° F. In a large bowl, mix together flour, sugar, baking powder, soda, and almonds. In a separate container, mix buttermilk, oil, and egg. Pour wet ingredients into dry and mix quickly with a fork until flour disappears. Do not overmix; batter should be lumpy. Spoon batter into greased muffin tins (3/4 full). Sprinkle each muffin with 1/2 teaspoon cinnamon/sugar mix. Bake 25 minutes.

La Maida House

North Hollywood, California

Fruit and vegetable rancher Antonio La Maida built this twenty-five-room Italian villa in 1926 with marble fireplace, spiral staircase, and bubbling fountains. And while the house saw the glamorous Hollywood of the 1930s and 1940s, today it has a star all its own: Megan Timothy, innkeeper, stained-glass artisan, photographer, and caterer admired by her peers for her creations of *edible* art.

Movie producers, directors, and celebrities are, nonetheless, numbered among La Maida's guest list, as the inn is in close proximity to the major studios—NBC, Warner Brothers, Universal, and Columbia—to name a few.

EGGS CROUSTADE

Serves six

6 large individual brioche
1 clove garlic, pressed
1/4 pound butter, melted

CHEESE SAUCE
3 tablespoons butter
3 tablespoons flour
1 teaspoon dry mustard
1/4 teaspoon salt
1/8 teaspoon ground white pepper
1 cup hot milk
3/4 cup grated sharp Cheddar cheese

6 eggs, softly poached
Finely chopped pimento
Finely chopped parsley

Preheat oven to 250° F. Slice the tops off the brioche to make "lids" and set aside. Carefully hollow out the center of each brioche, leaving a smooth shell. Add pressed garlic to melted butter. Using a pastry brush, brush brioche shells (inside and out) and lids (top and bottom) with garlic butter. Place on a baking sheet and bake 30–35 minutes, until light golden brown.

CHEESE SAUCE Melt butter in a saucepan over medium heat. Stir in flour; cook for just a minute, taking care not to brown. Stir in dry mustard, salt and pepper. Turn flame to low and slowly add the milk, stirring constantly to keep the sauce smooth. Cook until thick and bubbly. Add cheese and continue stirring until completely integrated into sauce. Keep the sauce warm while you quickly poach the eggs.

ASSEMBLY Place a tablespoon of the warm sauce in the bottom of each brioche shell. Set a poached egg down in the shell. Cover egg with as much sauce as the shell will hold. Garnish with finely chopped pimento and parsley. Top with brioche lid, or set the lid up on its side against the brioche shell. Serve immediately.

EGGS LA MAIDA

Serves six
2 tablespoons butter
1 cup freshly grated Parmesan cheese
6 eggs
3 tablespoons freshly whipped cream (optional)
2 tablespoons finely chopped fresh basil
Salt and pepper to taste

Preheat oven to 350° F. Grease a 7x10-inch glass baking dish with butter. Dust with as much of the grated cheese as will adhere to the buttered dish; set aside and reserve all excess cheese. Have a muffin tin ready for use. Separate the eggs, dropping the whites into a large mixing bowl and leaving each yolk, intact, in an eggshell half. Stand the eggshell halves upright in the muffin tin cups. Beat egg whites until they form stiff peaks. Gently, but quickly, fold in freshly whipped cream, basil, remaining Parmesan cheese, and salt and pepper to taste. Pour mixture into prepared pan and smooth top. Using the back of a tablespoon make 6 indentations in the egg whites. Slide an egg yolk into each indentation. Cover dish with a tent of foil. Bake until yolks are set, approximately 12–15 minutes. Remove foil. Turn oven temperature to broil. Slide under broiler for 1 minute, until egg whites are slightly browned. Serve at once.

CARROT MAPLE MUFFINS

Makes one dozen

1-1/2 cups sifted all-purpose flour
1/2 cup whole-wheat flour
2 teaspoons baking powder
1/2 teaspoon baking soda
Dash salt
1 large egg
1 cup milk
3 tablespoons vegetable oil
1/3 cup maple syrup
2/3 cup grated carrots

Preheat oven to 400° F. In a large bowl, mix together all-purpose flour, whole-wheat flour, baking powder, soda, and salt; set aside. In a smaller bowl, beat egg slightly. Add milk, oil, and maple syrup; stir until blended. Add grated carrots to dry ingredients; toss lightly. Pour in egg mixture and stir until just blended. Spoon into greased muffin tins (2/3 full). Bake 15 minutes.

OATMEAL BISCUITS

Makes one dozen

1-3/4 cups sifted all-purpose flour
1/3 cup rolled oats
1/4 teaspoon salt
1 teaspoon baking powder
1/2 teaspoon baking soda
4 tablespoons chilled sweet butter
3/4 cup buttermilk

Preheat oven to 400° F. Grease and flour a baking sheet. Combine flour, oats, salt, baking powder and soda in a bowl; mix thoroughly. Cut in chilled butter with pastry blender or knives. Process with fingertips until the mixture resembles coarse meal. Make a well in the center; pour in cold buttermilk. Mix to make a soft dough. (Dough will be quite dry; do not add more liquid.) Turn out onto lightly floured board and knead for about half a minute. Dough should be kept as cool as possible; do not overhandle. Roll out to 1/2-inch thickness and cut into rounds. Transfer to greased and floured baking sheet. Bake 15–20 minutes, until tops are golden brown.

The Fleming Jones Homestead

Placerville, California

This delightful farmhouse was the first bed and breakfast to open in the Sierra foothills of El Dorado County. But The Fleming Jones Homestead is a working farm as well as an inn. Proprietor Janice Condit raises chickens and sells the eggs (along with her homemade preserves). She lives in a converted milk house adjacent to the property, while her guests spend the night in the farmhouse or the bunk house, where lanterns, farm implements, and homestead treasures create the decor. Rocking chairs are plentiful here, as are rose bushes and vegetable gardens. Fruits from the orchards complement the homestead's expanded Continental breakfast with an emphasis on wholesome, farm-fresh foods.

THE FLEMING JONES HOMESTEAD BREAKFAST

Orange Juice with Ollalieberries

Baked Apples

Homestead Bran Muffins
with Orange Butter

Homestead Pumpkin Bread

French Roast Coffee
with Generous Dashes of Cinnamon

Herb Teas

HOMESTEAD BRAN MUFFINS

Makes sixteen muffins
3 cups All-Bran cereal
3/4 cup boiling water
1 heaping tablespoon frozen orange juice concentrate
1/2 cup vegetable oil
2 eggs, slightly beaten
2-1/2 cups all-purpose flour
1-1/2 cups sugar
2-1/2 teaspoons baking soda
2 cups buttermilk
1 cup currants
Ground walnuts or pecans
Orange Butter, following

Preheat oven to 350° F. Stir together 1 cup All-Bran, boiling water, orange juice, and oil. Add eggs and set aside. Combine flour, sugar, and baking soda. Stir in buttermilk and cereal/egg mixture. Add remaining 2 cups All-Bran and currants. Mix well. Spoon into greased muffin tins (2/3 full). Sprinkle ground nuts on top of each muffin. Bake 15–20 minutes. Serve with Orange Butter.

ORANGE BUTTER

Makes approximately one cup
1/4 pound butter
One 3-ounce package cream cheese
1/3 cup powdered sugar
2 tablespoons grated orange rind
1 tablespoon frozen orange juice concentrate

Bring butter and cream cheese to room temperature. Beat all ingredients with an electric mixer, or vigorously by hand, until smooth. Serve at room temperature. Store in refrigerator. If crumbly, bring back to room temperature and beat again.

HOMESTEAD PUMPKIN BREAD

Makes two loaves
1-2/3 cups all-purpose flour
1-1/2 cups sugar
1/4 teaspoon baking powder
1 teaspoon baking soda
1/2 teaspoon ground cloves
1/2 teaspoon ground cinnamon
1/2 teaspoon ground nutmeg
1/4 teaspoon ground allspice
1/2 cup vegetable oil
1/2 cup water
1 cup canned or steamed and puréed fresh pumpkin
2 eggs
1 cup chopped dates
1 cup chopped walnuts
1 cup currants (optional)

Preheat oven to 350° F. Mix together flour, sugar, baking powder, soda, and spices; set aside. Combine oil, water, pumpkin, and eggs in a separate mixing bowl. Add liquids to dry ingredients; mix thoroughly until blended. Fold in dates, walnuts, and currants. Spoon batter into 2 oiled 9x5-inch loaf pans (2/3 full). Bake 50–60 minutes or until toothpick inserted into center of bread comes out clean. Cool in pans; turn out onto a wire rack.

The Glenborough Inn

Santa Barbara, California

Heirlooms and old lace set the tone of this lovely bed and breakfast in Santa Barbara. There's the main house, a California bungalow, with four guest rooms, and an early 1880s cottage just across the street with an additional four. "Most of our guests come here for privacy," relates Glenborough owner Pat Hardy. "And romance!" partner Jo Ann Bell is quick to add. Amenities worth noting: a hot tub that can be reserved for private use, complimentary hors d'oeuvre, and breakfast delivered to your door.

LAZY WINTER MORNING BREAKFAST AT THE GLENBOROUGH INN

Orange Raspberry Juice

Yummy Baked Apples

Pat's Rich Date Nut Bread

Moma's Little Egg Casseroles

Glenborough Coffee

YUMMY BAKED APPLES

Per serving:
1 apple
1/4 cup raisins
Pinch ground cloves
Dash ground nutmeg
Dash ground cinnamon
Pinch ground dried orange peel
1/4 teaspoon brown sugar
1/4 teaspoon butter
Reconstituted orange juice
Sour cream

The night before serving, core apples and set upright in crockpot, Dutch oven, or 4-1/2-quart stockpot. In the center of each apple, layer raisins, cloves, nutmeg, cinnamon, orange peel, brown sugar, and butter. Pour reconstituted orange juice (fresh orange juice does not work) to fill pot up to the middle of apples. Cook in crockpot on low or in 200° F. oven overnight. Serve with a dollop of sour cream.

PAT'S RICH DATE NUT BREAD

Makes two loaves

1-1/2 cups boiling water
1-1/2 cups raisins
1-1/2 cups chopped dates
4 tablespoons butter
2-1/4 teaspoons baking soda
2-2/3 cups all-purpose flour
1-1/2 cups sugar
3/4 teaspoon salt
3 eggs
1-1/2 teaspoons vanilla extract
3/4 cup chopped walnuts

Preheat oven to 350° F. Pour boiling water over raisins, dates, butter, and baking soda. In a large mixing bowl, combine flour, sugar, and salt. Stir in raisin/date mixture. Add eggs, vanilla and nuts; mix well. Divide batter between 2 oiled 9x5-inch loaf pans. Bake 50–60 minutes.

MOMA'S LITTLE EGG CASSEROLES

Per serving:

1 slice bread
Pinch oregano
1/2 teaspoon diced mild green chili peppers
1/4 cup milk
1 egg
1/3 cup grated sharp Cheddar cheese
1/3 cup grated Monterey Jack cheese
Avocado slices
Sour cream

The night before serving, grease individual ramekins. Fit a slice of bread down in ramekin, trimming edges as necessary. Sprinkle with oregano and diced chilies. Whisk together milk and egg and pour over bread. Top with cheeses. Refrigerate overnight. Preheat oven to 350° F. Bake 30 minutes. Top with avocado slices and sour cream.

The Cinnamon Bear

St. Helena, California

Genny Jenkins purchased this California bungalow in 1971 to provide a home for her three growing children. Ten years later, with the last child out of the nest, she remodeled, changed the locks, and hung out her sign: The Cinnamon Bear Bed and Breakfast Inn. There was a little more to it than that, of course, but practically from the start the venture was a success. Needless to say, bears of all sizes and types preside over the inn's guest rooms, located on the second floor of the house. Breakfast is served in the dining room or on the front porch, as the weather allows.

THE CINNAMON BEAR'S
"BARELY SOUTH-OF-THE-BORDER"
BREAKFAST

Platter of Fresh Fruits

Hot Zucchini Bread

Corn and Cheese Muffins

Chili Egg Puff

Coffee with a Hint of Cinnamon

Tea

ZUCCHINI BREAD

Makes two loaves

2 cups sugar
3 cups all-purpose flour
1 tablespoon baking soda
1 teaspoon baking powder
1 teaspoon salt
1 tablespoon ground cinnamon
1 cup vegetable oil
3 eggs
1/4 cup buttermilk
2 tablespoons vanilla extract
3 cups grated zucchini
1 cup chopped walnuts

Preheat oven to 350° F. Combine sugar, flour, soda, baking powder, salt, and cinnamon in a large mixing bowl. Mix together oil, eggs, buttermilk, and vanilla. Add liquids to dry ingredients and mix well. Stir in zucchini and walnuts. Divide batter between 2 lightly oiled 9x5-inch pans. Bake 45 minutes. Turn out on a wire rack to cool.

CHILI EGG PUFF

Serves four

One 4-ounce can diced mild green chili peppers
1 cup grated Monterey Jack cheese
1 cup grated mild Cheddar cheese
8 eggs
1 cup milk
2 tablespoons Bisquick (optional)
Salsa
Sour cream

Preheat oven to 350° F. Evenly distribute diced chilies in the bottom of an ungreased 8x8-inch glass baking dish. Cover with cheeses. Whisk together eggs, milk, and Bisquick; pour over chili/cheese mix. Bake 40 minutes. Serve with salsa and sour cream.

The Foxes

Sutter Creek, California

Pete and Min Fox started innkeeping with just one luxury suite located on the top floor of their two-story Victorian, which doubled as the couple's private residence, antiques shop, and real estate office. Their first guests—honeymooners inadvertently left out in the cold by a neighboring inn on their wedding night—haven't failed to return for their anniversary in the five years since.

Today, however, the inn houses five suites and many more happy couples as part of its regular clientele. The pièce de résistance among the Foxes' many fine furnishings is a carved walnut bed with nine-foot-high headboard and matching marble-topped dresser, circa 1875. Just as irresistible are Min's Nutty Apple Coconut Muffins, heretofore found only in this part of California's Gold Country. Using the following recipe they now can be available in your kitchen as well.

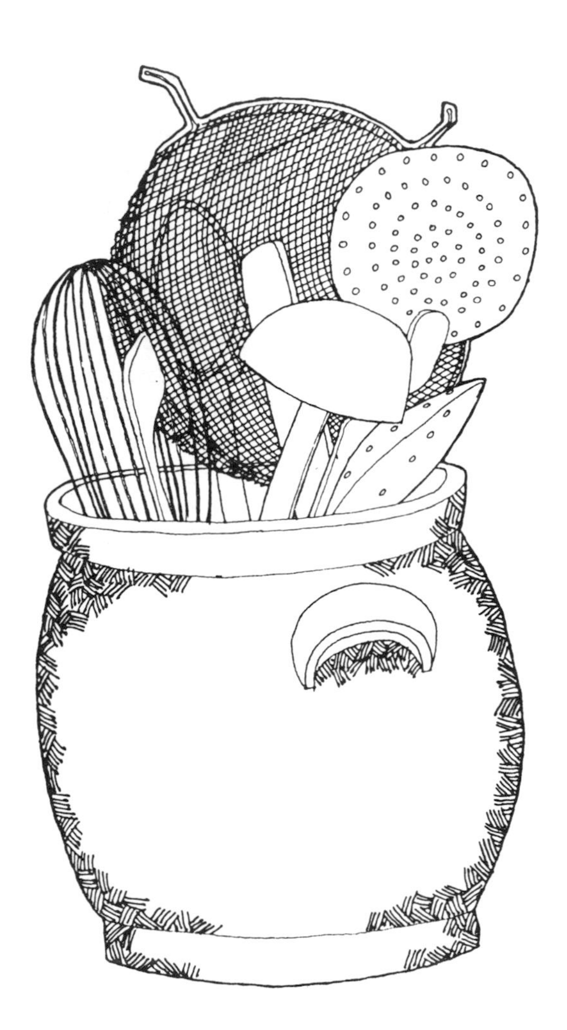

NUTTY APPLE COCONUT MUFFINS

Makes one dozen muffins

1 cup all-purpose flour
1/2 teaspoon salt
1 teaspoon baking soda
2 cups peeled, diced Golden Delicious apples
1 egg
1/4 cup vegetable oil
3/4 cup sugar
1 teaspoon freshly grated nutmeg
1 cup coarsely chopped walnuts
1/2 cup shredded coconut
Powdered sugar (optional)

Preheat oven to 350° F. Mix flour, salt, and baking soda together. In a separate bowl, add remaining ingredients and mix well. Add flour and blend until just moistened. Spoon batter into greased muffin tins (3/4 full) and bake 30–35 minutes. Let rest in pan several minutes before turning out. Dust with powdered sugar, if desired.

THE PACIFIC NORTHWEST

Romeo Inn

Campus Cottage

Marjon

Pillars by the Sea

Sally's Bed & Breakfast Manor

Inn of the White Salmon

Grouse Mountain
Bed & Breakfast

Heritage House

Romeo Inn

Ashland, Oregon

Cape Cod, Shakespeare, and a western mountain town? Yes, they all come together at the Romeo Inn, located a short walk from downtown Ashland and the Shakespearean Festival theaters. Standing at the crest of a carpet-like lawn, the fifty-year-old New England-style house is set amid big pines on land overlooking the mountains and valley. Four bedrooms are furnished with king-sized beds, private baths, easy chairs, and such sybaritic extras as robes and hot water bottles.

Retired airline pilot Anthony Romeo and his wife Patricia share more than their home. Tony is available as a tennis partner, and Pat prepares the hearty meals the inn is noted for. Fresh-baked breads, crêpes, and fruit are served for breakfast in the dining room or outdoors on the patio. Tea is set out in the late afternoon, and if that largesse weren't sufficient—cooking classes are offered each May.

ROMEO AND JULIET STRAWBERRY CREPES

Makes sixteen six-inch crêpes

CREPES
1 cup cold water
1 cup cold milk
4 eggs
1/2 teaspoon salt
2 cups all-purpose flour
4 tablespoons butter, melted

FILLING
Two 8-ounce packages cream cheese
1 pint sour cream
3/4 cup powdered sugar

SAUCE
2 cups fresh strawberries
1/2 cup sugar

TOPPING
3–4 cups lightly sweetened whole strawberries
Dollops of sour cream

CREPES Mix all ingredients in blender until smooth. Refrigerate at least 2 hours. Heat lightly oiled skillet, griddle or crêpe pan. Spoon 3–4 tablespoons batter into pan; lift and tilt to form 6-inch crêpe. Brown lightly on one side. Cool and stack between layers of waxed paper. Set aside.

FILLING Beat cream cheese, sour cream, and powdered sugar together with an electric mixer. Set aside.

SAUCE Crush strawberries and mix thoroughly with sugar.

ASSEMBLY Preheat oven to 350° F. Spread room temperature crêpes with 3–4 tablespoons of cream cheese filling. Roll and place seam side down in a 9x13-inch baking dish. Heat for 5–7 minutes. Remove from oven and top with sauce, whole strawberries, and dollops of sour cream.

Campus Cottage

Eugene, Oregon

Ursula Bates purchased the bungalow in 1981, some fifty years after it had been built as a private residence. Calling on a personal store of imagination and discernment, she transformed the vintage cottage into a country-fresh guest house with an atmosphere all its own.

Situated just a few blocks from the University of Oregon, Campus Cottage sits on Fraternity Row, convenient for university visitors and close to downtown Eugene.

Eugene's first B&B, Campus Cottage has two guest rooms furnished with antiques and comforter-plump beds; both have private baths. The Suite has a sitting room area complete with a twin Jenny Lind bed and giant fern. The Guestroom has a sinfully comfortable reading chair by the window and a cedar-lined shower.

Each morning fresh coffee is set out in the hall, and breakfasts of fruits, homemade pastries, and fancy egg dishes are served either in the living room or in the guest rooms.

COTTAGE BAKED EGGS

Serves four

5 eggs
1/4 cup all-purpose flour
1/2 teaspoon baking powder
3/4 cup cottage cheese
8 ounces Monterey Jack cheese, grated
1/2 pound bulk sausage, sautéed and crumbled
1/2 cup sliced fresh mushrooms

Preheat oven to 375° F. Beat eggs with a fork or wire whisk. Add flour and baking powder; mix well. Stir in remaining ingredients. Pour into a buttered 8x8-inch baking dish. Bake 20 minutes. Serve immediately.

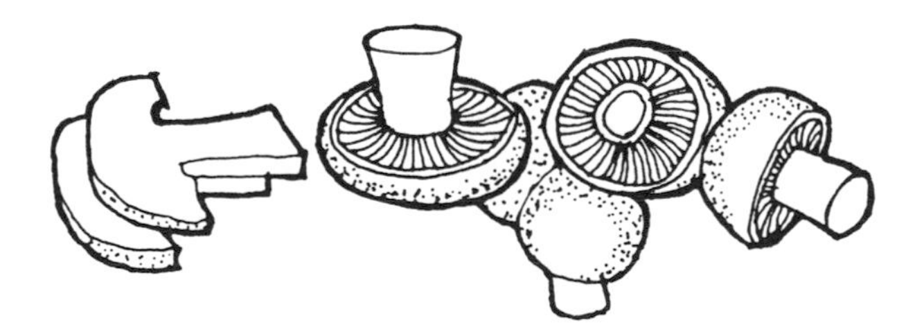

Marjon

Leaburg, Oregon

Located twenty-four miles east of Eugene, the contemporary cedar chalet of Marjon nestles in green forest at the edge of the McKenzie River. Surrounding the house are sweeping lawns, ferns, azaleas, rhododendrons, a creek, and a one-hundred-year-old apple tree. These natural wonders are as captivating as their owner: Countess Margaret Olga Von Retzlaff Haas.

Don't let the title intimidate you. Guests partake in Margie's hospitality in a comfortable living room dominated by a massive hearthstone fireplace enhanced with exquisite Oriental accessories. A glass wall looks toward the river, and sliding doors lead to the covered terrace where breakfast is served.

Two rooms are available. The Master Suite features a sunken tub with a view of the Japanese garden; the Guest Room has a unique "fishbowl shower" with views of the river.

Marjon's full breakfast includes hand-sculptured fresh fruit under glass, warm popovers, and aebleskivers with fresh banana centers.

AEBLESKIVERS

Makes fourteen to sixteen

1-1/2 cups all-purpose flour
2 teaspoons baking powder
1/2 teaspoon salt
3 eggs
1 cup milk
3 tablespoons butter, melted
1 large banana, sliced into 16 1/2-inch pieces
Maple syrup, heated

Combine flour, baking powder, and salt. Slightly beat eggs; stir in milk and butter. Add to flour; mix until thoroughly blended. Heat a lightly oiled aebleskiver pan.* Fill holes half full of batter and cook over medium heat until brown on the bottom (small bubbles will form around edges of batter) 2–3 minutes. Drop a piece of banana into each aebleskiver before turning with a fork. Cook an additional 2–3 minutes. Serve immediately with hot maple syrup.

**Aebleskiver pans are available in gourmet cookware stores*

Pillars by the Sea

Freeland, Whidbey Island, Washington

Tongue-and-groove cedar pillars lend their name to this 1907 bungalow on Whidbey Island. Home of retired Methodist minister Walker Jordon and his wife Ellen, the two-guest-room inn is appointed with family heirlooms, antique dolls, and Oriental carpets. Of particular interest is the cranberry glass Ellen has collected through the years.

China, crystal, and silver grace the dining table where guests are treated to soul satisfying breakfasts of sour cream eggs à la crêpe with bacon and freshly baked date-nut muffins or the Jordon's special Corn-Apple Hotcakes with ham and eggs. As one contented guest put it to Walker: "You're not really retired, just ministering in a different way."

CORN-APPLE HOTCAKES

Makes eight six-inch hotcakes

2/3 cup yellow cornmeal
1-1/3 cups all-purpose flour
1/4 cup sugar
1 teaspoon salt
2 teaspoons baking powder
1 teaspoon baking soda
1/8 teaspoon ground allspice
1 large apple, peeled, cored, and chopped
3 eggs
1/4 pound butter, melted
1-1/2 cups buttermilk
Maple syrup

Sift together cornmeal, flour, sugar, salt, baking powder, soda, and allspice. Stir in chopped apple and set aside. Whisk together eggs, butter, and buttermilk. Add wet ingredients to dry; mix thoroughly. Let stand 15–20 minutes. Pour or ladle 1/3 cup batter onto a hot, lightly oiled griddle. Cook until small bubbles appear on the surface and the edges turn dry. Flip hotcake and cook other side. Repeat to make 8 hotcakes. Serve with butter and maple syrup.

Sally's Bed & Breakfast Manor

Langley, Whidbey Island, Washington

Sally's Bed & Breakfast Manor is accessible only by ferry from Mukilteo to Whidbey Island. This home-turned-inn of proprietor Sally De Felice is situated on three scenic acres overlooking the Cascades and Puget Sound's Saratoga Passage. The traditional furnishings which fill the inn, the fieldstone fireplace which warms the living room, and two guest suites with interiors running along a "country elegance" theme are conducive to quiet reading, writing, and reflective moments looking out to mountains and sea.

A hearty breakfast appears in the sunroom at a leisurely hour. The dish of choice is Sally's Special Egg Casserole, complemented by Spiced Bran Muffins, homemade yogurt, and fresh fruits.

SALLY'S SPECIAL

Orange Juice

Cantaloupe with Yogurt and Strawberries

Spiced Bran Muffins

Sally's Special Egg Casserole

Coffee and Tea

SPICED BRAN MUFFINS

Makes three dozen muffins

One 15-ounce box raisin bran cereal
1-1/2 cups sugar
2 cups whole-wheat flour
3 cups all-purpose flour
5 teaspoons baking soda
1 teaspoon baking powder
2 teaspoons salt
1 teaspoon ground cinnamon
1/2 teaspoon ground ginger
1/2 teaspoon ground allspice
1 cup vegetable oil
4 eggs
1 quart buttermilk
2 tablespoons light molasses

In a large mixing bowl, combine cereal, sugar, flour, soda, baking powder, salt, cinnamon, ginger, and allspice. In a smaller mixing bowl, mix oil, eggs, buttermilk, and molasses. Add wet ingredients to dry and mix thoroughly. Let batter sit 30 minutes. Preheat oven to 400° F. Spoon batter into greased muffin tins (3/4 full). Bake 15 minutes.

SALLY'S SPECIAL EGG CASSEROLE

Serves eight

12 eggs
6 tablespoons plain yogurt
6–8 tablespoons medium-hot tomato salsa*
1 pound bulk pork sausage
1 medium onion, chopped
6 ounces fresh mushrooms, sliced
8 ounces Cheddar cheese, grated
8 ounces mozzarella cheese, grated

Preheat oven to 350° F. Blend eggs and yogurt together with a wire whisk or in a food processor. Pour into a greased 9x13-inch baking dish. Bake 15 minutes, or until eggs are set. Remove from oven and cool slightly. Drizzle with salsa and set aside. Reduce oven temperature to 300° F. Crumble and cook sausage in a frying pan; drain and return to heat. Add onion and mushrooms; sauté until limp. Spoon over eggs and salsa. Top with cheeses. Bake 25–30 minutes, until bubbly.

**The innkeeper recommends La Victoria Salsa Supreme*

Inn of the White Salmon

White Salmon, Washington

When the Hoppers were trying to find ways to improve the quality of guest lodgings at their newly purchased Inn of the White Salmon, Bill said: "Coffee and rolls would be nice, Loretta." That was six years ago. Today, Loretta is justly famous for her "coffee and rolls"—a buffet breakfast that includes thirty-eight different homemade pastries, seven unusual egg dishes, five fruits of the season, three fruit juices, and a selection of hot beverages (hot spiced cider, steaming hot chocolate, freshly roasted coffee, and tea) *every day!* And, the inevitable question: What happens to the leftovers? "We're pretty popular with the neighbors," Loretta replies. Surely all two thousand of them, which is the approximate population of the town of White Salmon. Besides eating, wind surfing, water-skiing, snow skiing, hiking, hunting, and fishing are activities enjoyed by natives and tourists alike.

ARTICHOKE FRITTATA

Serves four to six

One 8-ounce can artichoke hearts
2 tablespoons butter
1/2 cup grated Parmesan cheese
10 eggs
3/4 cup half-and-half
1-1/2 cups grated Monterey Jack cheese

Preheat oven to 350° F. Drain artichoke hearts and cut into quarters. Melt butter in a skillet. Add artichokes and sauté until coated with butter and heated through. Distribute artichokes evenly in the bottom of an 8x8-inch baking dish. Sprinkle with 1/4 cup of the grated Parmesan (reserve remaining 1/4 cup of cheese). In a small mixing bowl beat eggs together with half-and-half. Pour over artichokes. Sprinkle the Monterey Jack cheese over entire mixture. Bake 30 minutes. Remove from oven and sprinkle reserved Parmesan over frittata. Return to oven for an additional 5 minutes. Serve hot.

APRICOT JAM STRUDEL

Makes twelve servings

DOUGH
1 cup all-purpose flour
1/4 teaspoon salt
1/4 pound butter
1/2 cup sour cream

FILLING
3/4 cup apricot jam
1/2 cup white raisins
3/4 cup shredded coconut
2/3 cup chopped walnuts

Powdered sugar

DOUGH Combine flour and salt. Cut in butter with a pastry blender or knives until mixture resembles coarse meal. Blend in sour cream. Cover and refrigerate at least 1 hour and up to 1 week.

ASSEMBLY Preheat oven to 350° F. Roll out dough on a floured board to 10x15 inches. Spread with apricot jam, leaving a 1/2-inch border around the edge of dough. Sprinkle with raisins, coconut, and walnuts. Roll up lengthwise. Pinch seam; tuck edges under. Place seam-side-down on an ungreased baking sheet. Bake 30–35 minutes. Cool slightly. Dust with powdered sugar. Best when served warm.

Grouse Mountain Bed & Breakfast

North Vancouver, British Columbia

After ten years of traveling the world, staying at B&Bs along the way, John and Lyne Armstrong decided to open an inn of their own. They are now busy hosting foreign and domestic guests in their contemporary two-story home in the foothills of Grouse Mountain, with Vancouver a quick ten minutes away. There are two rooms for guests, each with private entrance. One has a cedar-paneled bath, the other a flagstone fireplace. A heroic, full-course breakfast—juice, cereal, eggs and bacon, toast with homemade jam, a pot of coffee—is served each morning.

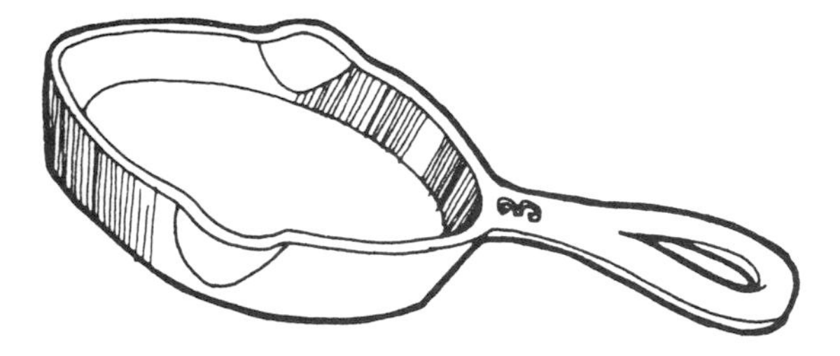

DIVINE FILLED CROISSANTS

Serves four

4 croissants
4 tablespoons butter
8 eggs
1/4 cup milk
1 teaspoon dried basil
1/2 cup chopped mushrooms
1/2 cup grated Monterey Jack cheese
4 orange slices
Parsley sprigs

Preheat oven to 250° F. Warm croissants in oven. Meanwhile, melt butter in a frying pan. Beat together eggs and milk, pour into pan, and scramble until creamy. Add basil and mushrooms to egg mixture and heat through. Slice croissants (so they open like a clam shell) about 3/4 of the way through. Fill with scrambled egg mixture, sprinkle with cheese, and stick under the broiler until the cheese is just melted. Garnish with orange twists and sprigs of parsley.

Heritage House

Victoria, British Columbia

Heritage House—a miniature Stick-style Victorian mansion with gabled roofs—was built in 1910. Doreen and Irvin Stang came upon it on a trip from Calgary in 1979, saw its potential as an inn, and made their choice. They've had no regrets.

Three miles from downtown Victoria, the house rests quietly in a setting of lawns and flower beds, oaks, and firs. Its five guest rooms accommodate a fine collection of family antiques and brass beds.

"We offer breakfast like Mom used to cook—farm-fresh eggs, lots of porridge, and homemade blackberry or bran muffins," says Doreen. "While it may not be fancy, it's good, and there's plenty of it."

In order to have everything ready on time, Doreen starts fixing breakfast early over the kitchen's wood stove. But guests have until eight to settle down in the walnut-paneled dining room.

SURPRISE BRAN MUFFINS

Makes four dozen muffins

4 cups all-purpose flour
2 cups sugar
4 teaspoons baking soda
2 teaspoons salt
4 cups unprocessed bran
3 eggs
4 cups milk
1-1/2 cups vegetable oil
One 8-ounce package cream cheese

Preheat oven to 425° F. In a large bowl, mix flour, sugar, baking soda, salt, and bran; set aside. Beat together eggs, milk, and oil. Add wet ingredients to dry and mix until just blended. (This mixture will keep in refrigerator for up to 2 weeks.) To bake, spoon batter into greased muffin tins (3/4 full) and place a 1/2-inch square piece of cream cheese in center of each muffin. Bake 15–20 minutes.

Preserving Techniques

EQUIPMENT Use a flat-bottomed kettle made of stainless steel, aluminum, or heavy enamel; do not use iron, tin, or copper. Other helpful equipment includes long-handled wooden spoons, a wide-mouthed funnel, and stainless steel tongs. For processing in a hot water bath, you should have a jar-lifter. The recipes in this book and the following general method apply to a self-sealing lid.

FILLING AND SEALING With tongs remove one jar at a time from kettle, tipping to drain well. Using a sterilized wide-mouthed funnel, ladle in jam or jelly. Leave 1/8-inch headroom to the top of the jar. With a clean, damp cloth, carefully wipe off the rim of the jar to remove any food particles. Using tongs lift out lids, tip to drain, place on top of jar and tighten screw top.

HOT WATER BATH PROCESS If recipe calls for processing jars in a hot water bath, you will need a kettle with rack and tight-fitting lid, large enough to hold jars with 2 inches of space between them and 2 inches of water to cover. Place sealed jars on rack in kettle; being careful not to pour water directly on tops of jar lids, pour in water to cover jars. Bring to a boil, cover, and boil lightly for the time specified in recipe. Start timing when water comes to a boil. If processing time is lengthy, add boiling water as needed to keep jars covered. Remove jars from water with jar-lifter and place in cool, draft-free area.

TESTING FOR SEAL After jars have been sealed and processed (if called for), remove them to a cool, draft-free area. As they cool a vacuum should be created that will pull down the lid leaving a concave hollow on top. You will hear pings and pops as this occurs. About an hour after sealing, check jars by pressing down on lids; if lid pops back up, it is not sealed properly. In this case refrigerate immediately and use as soon as possible. Let remaining jars stand 12 hours. If you wish, rings may be removed at this point. Wipe jars clean, label with content and date, and store in a cool, dark place. Properly preserved foods keep without spoilage for up to one year.

PREPARATION OF EQUIPMENT All equipment, jars, and lids should be first washed in hot, soapy water; rinsed and drained. Jars should be examined carefully for nicks and cracks. In a pot of boiling water, scald spoons, funnel, measuring cups, tongs, ladles, and any other equipment you will be using. About an hour before filling jars, place them in a large kettle of boiling water to cover and boil at least 20 minutes; turn off heat and keep jars immersed in hot water until ready to fill. About 10 minutes ahead of time, place self-sealing lids in their rings (to facilitate removal) in a large saucepan. Cover with water, bring just to boiling point, turn off heat and keep in water until ready to use. Jars and lids should be hot when filled.

Recipe Index

FRUIT DISHES

JAMS, JELLIES, SPREADS

MAIN-COURSE EGG DISHES

MAIN DISHES

MISCELLANEOUS

Inn Directory

NEW ENGLAND

BUTTERNUT FARM   Page 3
1654 Main Street
Glastonbury, CT 06033
Innkeeper: Donald Reid
Telephone: (203) 633-7197

THE CAPTAIN JEFFERDS INN   Page 4
Pearl Street
Box 691
Kennebunkport, ME 04046
Innkeepers: Warren Fitzsimmons and Don Kelly
Telephone: (207) 967-2311

THE GOVERNOR'S INN   Page 13
86 Main Street
Ludlow, VT 05149
Innkeepers: Charlie and Deedy Marble
Telephone: (802) 228-8830

HAWTHORNE INN Page 7
462 Lexington Road
Concord, MA 01742
Innkeepers: Gregory Burch and Marilyn Mudry
Telephone: (617) 369-5610

HOLIDAY INN Page 9
Route 16-A
P.O. Box 37
Intervale, NH 03845
Innkeepers: Lynne and Jim Clough
Telephone: (603) 356-9772

THE INN AT MANCHESTER Page 15
Route 7-A
Box 41
Manchester, VT 05254
Innkeepers: Stan and Harriet Rosenberg
Telephone: (802) 362-1793

THE INN AT WESTON Page 16
Route 100
Weston, VT 05161
Innkeepers: Sue and Stu Douglas
Telephone: (802) 824-5804

WAYBURY INN Page 11
Route 125
East Middlebury, VT 05740
Innkeepers: Jim and Betty Riley
Telephone: (802) 388-4015

THE MID-ATLANTIC

ALEXANDER'S INN Page 21
653 Washington Street
Cape May, NJ 08204
Innkeepers: Larry and Diane Muentz
Telephone: (609) 884-2555

BARNARD-GOOD HOUSE Page 23
238 Perry Street
Cape May, NJ 08204
Innkeepers: Nan and Tom Hawkins
Telephone: (609) 884-5381

CAPTAIN MEY'S INN Page 27
202 Ocean Street
Cape May, NJ 08204
Innkeepers: Milly LaCanfora
and Carin Feddermann
Telephone: (609) 884-7793 or 884-9637

THE MAINSTAY INN Page 29
635 Columbia Avenue
Cape May, NJ 08204
Innkeepers: Tom and Sue Carroll
Telephone: (609) 884-8690

THE QUEEN VICTORIA Page 31
102 Ocean Street
Cape May, NJ 08204
Innkeepers: Joan and Dane Wells
Telephone: (609) 884-8702

THE SUMMER COTTAGE INN   Page 34
613 Columbia Avenue
P.O. Box 27
Cape May, NJ 08204
Innkeepers: Bill and Nancy Rishforth
Telephone: (609) 884-4948

THE WEDGWOOD INN   Page 37
111 West Bridge Street
New Hope, PA 18938
Innkeepers: Carl Glassman
and Nadine Silnutzer
Telephone: (215) 862-2570

THE SOUTH

THE BURN   Page 47
712 North Union Street
Natchez, MI 39120
Innkeepers: Tony and Loretta Byrne
Telephone: (601) 445-8566 or 442-1344

THE CONYERS HOUSE   Page 52
Slate Mills Road
Sperryville, VA 22740
Innkeepers: Sandra and Norman Cartwright-Brown
Telephone: (703) 987-8025

DEVON COTTAGE   Page 43
26 Eureka Street
Eureka Springs, AR 72632
Innkeeper: Laura Menees
Telephone: (501) 253-9169

FOLKESTONE LODGE   Page 51
Route 1, Box 310
West Deep Creek Road
Bryson City, NC 28713
Innkeeper: Mary Briggs
Telephone: (704) 488-2730

THE GREYSTONE INN   Page 45
24 East Jones Street
Savannah, GA 31401
Innkeeper: Woody Cunningham
Telephone: (912) 236-2442

OAK SQUARE   Page 49
1207 Church Street
Port Gibson, MI 39150
Innkeepers: Martha and William Lum
Telephone: (601) 437-4350

THE MIDWEST

CANTERBURY INN   Page 64
723 Second Street S.W.
Rochester, MN 55902
Innkeepers: Mary Martin and Jeffrey Van Sant
Telephone: (507) 289-5553

HAUS AUSTRIAN   Page 57
4626 Omena Point Road
Omena, MI 49674
Innkeeper: Chris Misangyi
Telephone: (616) 386-7338

THE RAHILLY HOUSE Page 62
304 Oak Street
Lake City, MN 55041
Innkeepers: Gary and Dorene Fechtmeyer
Telephone: (612) 345-4664

THORWOOD BED & BREAKFAST Page 60
649 West Third Street
Hastings, MN 55033
Innkeepers: Dick and Pam Thorsen
Telephone: (612) 437-3297

YOUNGS' ISLAND Page 58
Gunflint Trail 67-1
Grand Marais, MN 55604
Innkeepers: Barbara and Ted Young
Telephone: (218) 388-4487

THE SOUTHWEST

1899 INN Page 69
314 South Main
La Veta, CO 81055
Innkeeper: Marilyn Hall
Telephone: (303) 742-3576

GRANT CORNER INN Page 72
122 Grant Avenue
Santa Fe, NM 87501
Innkeepers: Pat and Louise Walter
Telephone: (505) 983-6678

THE OLD MINERS' LODGE Page 78
615 Woodside Avenue, Box 2639
Park City, UT 84060
Innkeepers: Hugh Daniels, Jeff Sadowsky and
Kathleen Johnson
Telephone: (801)645-8068

RANCHO ARRIBA Page 75
P.O. Box 338
Truchas, NM 87578
Innkeepers: Curtiss and Jessica Frank
Telephone: (505) 689-2374

TRAVELER'S HOTEL Page 77
300 East Main
Denison, TX 75020
Innkeepers: Bob and Betty Brandt
Telephone: (214) 465-2372

CALIFORNIA

THE BEAZLEY HOUSE Page 98
1910 First Street
Napa, CA 94559
Innkeepers: Jim and Carol Beazley
Telephone: (707) 257-1649

CAMPBELL RANCH INN Page 87
1475 Canyon Road
Geyserville, CA 95441
Innkeepers: Mary Jane and Jerry Campbell
Telephone: (707) 857-3476

CARTER HOUSE Page 84
1033 Third Street
Eureka, CA 95501
Innkeepers: Mark and Christi Carter
Telephone: (707) 445-1390

THE CINNAMON BEAR Page 108
1407 Kearney Street
St. Helena, CA 94574
Innkeeper: Genny Jenkins
Telephone: (707) 963-4653

THE FLEMING JONES HOMESTEAD Page 103
3170 Newtown Road
Placerville, CA 95667
Innkeeper: Janice Condit
Telephone: (916) 626-5840

THE FOXES Page 109
77 Main Street
P.O. Box 159
Sutter Creek, CA 95685
Innkeepers: Pete and Min Fox
Telephone: (209) 267-5882

THE GLENBOROUGH INN Page 105
1327 Bath Street
Santa Barbara, CA 93101
Innkeepers: Pat Hardy and Jo Ann Bell
Telephone: (805) 966-0589

GRAPE LEAF INN Page 94
539 Johnson Street
Healdsburg, CA 95448
Innkeepers: Terry Sweet and Kathy Cookson
Telephone: (707) 433-8140

THE GREY WHALE INN Page 86
615 North Main Street
Fort Bragg, CA 95437
Innkeepers: John and Colette Bailey
Telephone: (707) 964-0640

THE HEIRLOOM Page 96
214 Shakeley Lane
Ione, CA 95640
Innkeepers: Patricia Cross and Melisande Hubbs
Telephone: (209) 274-4468

HOPE-MERRILL HOUSE Page 90
21253 Geyserville Avenue
P.O. Box 42
Geyserville, CA 95441
Innkeepers: Bob and Rosalie Hope
Telephone: (707) 857-3356

LA MAIDA HOUSE Page 100
11159 La Maida Street
North Hollywood, CA 91601
Innkeeper: Megan Timothy
Telephone: (818) 769-3857

ROSE VICTORIAN INN Page 81
789 Valley Road
Arroyo Grande, CA 93420
Innkeepers: Diana and Ross Cox
Telephone: (805) 481-5566

SAN BENITO HOUSE Page 91
356 Main Street
Half Moon Bay, CA 94019
Innkeeper: Carol Mickelsen
Telephone: (415) 726-3425

THE PACIFIC NORTHWEST

CAMPUS COTTAGE Page 115
1136 East 19th Avenue
Eugene, OR 97403
Innkeeper: Ursula Bates
Telephone: (503) 342-5346

GROUSE MOUNTAIN BED & BREAKFAST
Page 122
900 Clements Avenue
North Vancouver, BC V7R 2K7
Innkeepers: John and Lyne Armstrong
Telephone: (604) 986-9630

HERITAGE HOUSE Page 123
1100 Brunside Road West
Victoria, BC V8Z 1N3
Innkeepers: Doreen and Irvin Stang
Telephone: (604) 479-8092

INN OF THE WHITE SALMON Page 120
172 West Jewett
P.O. Box 1446
White Salmon, WA 98672
Innkeepers: Bill and Loretta Hopper
Telephone: (509) 493-2335

MARJON Page 116
44975 Leaburg Dam Road
Leaburg, OR 97489
Innkeeper: Margie Haas
Telephone: (503) 896-3145

PILLARS BY THE SEA Page 117
1367 East Bayview Avenue
Freeland, WA 98249
Innkeepers: Walker and Ellen Jordon
Telephone: (206) 221-7738

ROMEO INN Page 113
295 Idaho Street
Ashland, OR 97520
Innkeepers: Anthony and Patricia Romeo
Telephone: (503) 488-0884

SALLY'S BED & BREAKFAST MANOR Page 118
215 Sixth Street
P.O. Box 459
Langley, Whidbey Island, WA 98260
Innkeeper: Sally De Felice
Telephone: (206) 221-8709

Linda Kay Bristow

Life seems to go in circles sometimes, and such was the case when Linda Kay Bristow found herself traveling, writing about inns, and collecting breakfast recipes.

In 1969, she graduated from a Midwestern high school with the Betty Crocker Homemaker of the Year award. While she never married or raised a family, as the honor might have implied, she did go on to graduate from MacMurray College in Jacksonville, Illinois, with a degree in Sociology in 1973 and then headed west.

In San Francisco working full time as a secretary by day and writing at night, she once again "graduated," but this time from newspaper articles to magazine feature stories to books.

Her first book, *Bed and Breakfast: California,* a travel guide, sold 10,000 copies the first six weeks it was out and has subsequently been revised.

The next major hurdle was what to do with the recipes for all those great breakfast dishes she'd tried while visiting inns. The logical answer was a bed and breakfast cookbook.

In *Bread & Breakfast,* the hundred and fifty or so recipes she tested from inns across the country proved that those homemaking skills, bread-baking methods, and canning techniques though dormant, were certainly not forgotten.